The Model in Practice

Using the EFQM Excellence Model to deliver continuous improvement

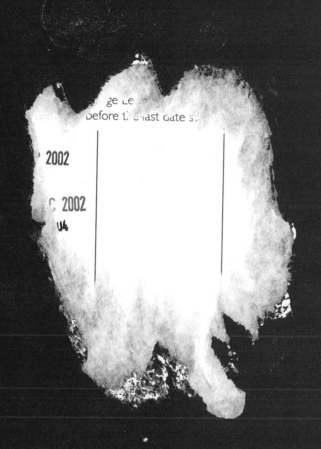

British Quality Foundation

First edition: September 2000

Copyright © 2000 belongs to
The British Quality Foundation.

EFQM Excellence Model is EFQM (European
Foundation for Quality Management)
Copyright © 1999.

It is EFQM's intent to encourage the
widespread use of this Model. However, no
part of the Model may be reproduced,
stored in a retrieval system, or
communicated in any form or by any
means (be this electronically, mechanically,
through photocopy or recording, or
otherwise) without the prior written
permission from EFQM.

Produced by Deer Park Productions.

Designed for
The British Quality Foundation by
Topics – The Creative Partnership
Exeter • Devon • EX2 6HD

Printed in Great Britain by
Ashford Colour Press

The Model in Practice

Using the EFQM Excellence Model to deliver continuous improvement

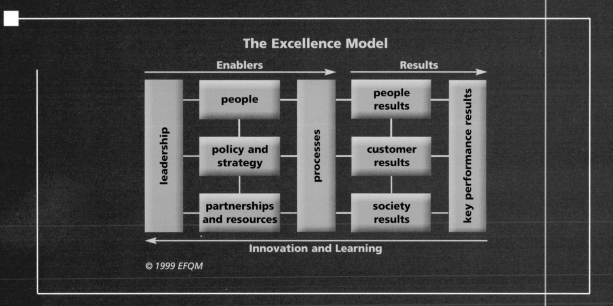

The Excellence Model

Enablers → Results →

- leadership
- people
- policy and strategy
- partnerships and resources
- processes
- people results
- customer results
- society results
- key performance results

Innovation and Learning ←

© 1999 EFQM

British Quality Foundation

Acknowledgements

> "If I have been able to see further than others, it is because I have stood on the shoulders of giants."
>
> Sir Isaac Newton

This book presents the results of a project set up to answer the question most often asked about the Excellence Model - "What does this look like in practice?" It therefore sets out to define the model and to offer examples of best practice across a range of sectors.

In the development of this book, we came across many examples of good and best practice, but could only choose a limited number to quote. We are hugely indebted to all those who agreed to allow us to use material from their organisations and to all those individuals who so willingly gave of their time and experiences. Without their help and encouragement this book would not have been possible. The book is all about best practice, and we have been fortunate in learning of such a diverse and interesting selection.

The research was carried out by the European Centre for Business Excellence – the research and education division of Oakland Consulting plc. The work was directed and produced by The British Quality Foundation and supported by the European Foundation for Quality Management.

From a cast of many dozens, the following people deserve special recognition for their contributions:

Origination: Joachim Bauer, Mary Davies and Steve Tanner.

Research, verification, co-ordination and production: Chris Carrington, Fiona Duffy, Ken Gadd, Lorraine Guyot, Ray Louden (Army School of Equipment Support), John Oakland, Les Porter, Diane Ritherdon and Robin Walker.

Once again, as with so much of the work of the BQF, an essential ingredient has been the inspiration and support of our networking groups and members to whom we are also as grateful as ever.

John Smith
August 2000

The British Quality Foundation
is a membership organisation set up in 1994 to promote Excellence througout the UK. To find out more about how membership can help you and your organisation – whether you are in the private or public sector, or from a large or small organisation – contact us on:

Telephone: + 44 (0) 20 7654 5000
Fax: + 44 (0) 20 7654 5001
E-mail: mail@quality-foundation.co.uk
Website: www.quality-foundation.co.uk

European Centre for Business Excellence

Telephone: + 44 (0) 113 234 1944
Fax: + 44 (0) 113 234 1988
E-mail: ecforbe@compuserve.com
Website: www.ecforbe.com

Contents

Chapter 1 | Introduction

1.1 About this Book

This book is for people from all sectors with one thing in common – you wish to improve the performance of your organisation and recognise that this can be achieved using the EFQM Excellence Model as a framework for this improvement. You do not need to have any previous experience of business excellence to understand and use this book for the benefit of your organisation.

All the data and examples in the book are from UK-based organisations (Appendix 1), and selected from research on the basis of being practical examples of the Excellence Model in use. The British Quality Foundation (BQF) acknowledges all the contributors, which include award winners and other exemplar organisations, and thanks them for sharing their practices.

This book will help you to understand the principles behind the Model, reinforced by examples of what is actually being done in a variety of organisations. Reading these examples, taken from private, public and small organisations, will inspire you to adopt and apply the Model within your own organisation. In addition, this book will be a valuable input to your business improvement planning activities, helping you to manage and measure them.

1.2 | The Fundamental Concepts of Excellence

Truly excellent organisations are measured by their ability to achieve and sustain outstanding results for all their stakeholders, such as customers, employees, shareholders and the community. This requires a management approach based on eight fundamental concepts:

Results Orientation: The needs of stakeholders are met and balanced. Stakeholders may include employees, customers, suppliers, shareholders and society.

Customer Focus: There is a clear understanding of the needs of both current and potential customers, and a passion for meeting needs and exceeding expectations.

Leadership and Constancy of Purpose: Leaders have a clear sense of direction and purpose, which they communicate effectively throughout the organisation.

Management by Process and Facts: All activities are managed in a systematic and effective way, taking into account all stakeholders' perceptions.

People Development and Involvement: A culture of trust and empowerment that allows all employees to develop and contribute to their full potential.

Continuous Learning, Improvement and Innovation: Knowledge is shared to maximise performance, with learning, innovation and improvement encouraged.

Partnership Development: There are mutually beneficial relationships with all partners.

Public Responsibility: The organisation fosters a positive and mutually beneficial relationship with society and the community.

N.B. There is no significance in the order of these concepts.

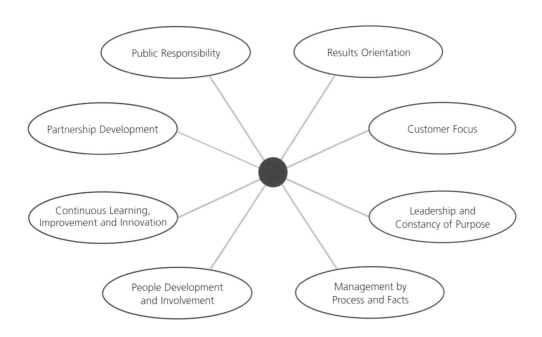

1.3 Driving Business Improvement Using the Model

The fundamental concepts behind the Model have been described previously, but the key question is 'How does the Model help drive business improvement?'

This is achieved through the application of RADAR® philosophy, which is at the heart of the Model. It consists of four elements:

The philosophy is that an organisation needs to:

- *Determine the **Results** it is aiming for from its policy and strategy*
- *Plan and develop an integrated set of **Approaches***
- ***Deploy** the approaches, then*
- ***Assess** and **Review** these approaches, to identify, prioritise, plan and implement improvements.*

The Excellence Model has nine criteria that are broken down into two main groups, enablers and results. The five enablers are the things an organisation does in order to achieve the desired results. This result/enabler breakdown provides a valuable way for you to classify your organisation's activities and performance.

The theme of innovation and learning spans the Model and reinforces the feedback mechanisms that drive the improvement in your organisation's performance.

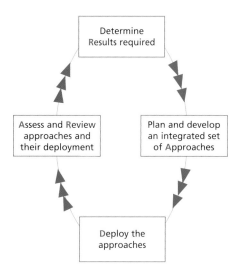

The Excellence Model

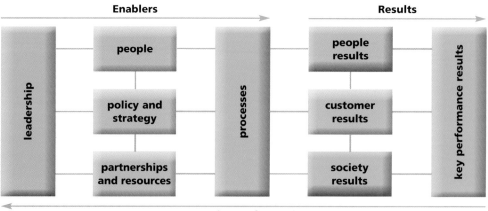

© 1999 EFQM. The Model is a registered trademark of EFQM

This book is structured around the nine criteria of the Model, and demonstrates the linkages between each of them, e.g. the ways in which the 'People' approaches drive the 'People' results.

1.4 | Benefits from Practising Excellence in Business

Business Excellence is not just another initiative, but a way of pulling several initiatives together in a focused and practical way. There is wide-ranging evidence from around the world that supports the benefits to be gained from following a philosophy of Excellence in business. This data comes from research into organisations that have won national and international Excellence awards, such as the UK Quality Award, the European Quality Award, the Japanese Deming Prize and the Malcolm Baldrige National Quality Award (MBNQA) in the USA.

It includes:

- Research, carried out by the European Centre for Business Excellence supported by the BQF and published in the 'X-Factor' report, reveals overwhelming verification of the links between Excellence, improved business performance and outstanding business results.

- A study of European companies using the concepts of Excellence showed that these companies out-performed their industry median, on four different financial indicators over a five-year period. For example, profit per employee in 79% of the companies was higher, 76% of the companies had a higher return on assets and 76% of the companies showed higher profit margins than their industry medians.

- The US National Institute of Standards and Technology hypothetically invested in $1000 of stock in each of the publicly traded American Baldrige Award winners over a seven-year period. These stocks outperformed the Standard and Poor's 500 (equivalent to the FTSE 100) index by between 3 and 3.5 to 1.

- A study of the Japanese Deming Prize-winners between 1961 and 1980 concluded that most companies had an upward trend in all key performance indicators and maintained this performance above the industry average.

(refer to Appendix 2 for references).

1.5 Chapter 3 Layout

Chapter 3 of this book is divided into sections according to the nine criteria of the Model, and each section is introduced by the definition of that criterion and its sub-criteria, plus an illustration of linkages between the sub-criteria within that criterion, and between all the enabler criteria.

Each of the nine sections then examines the sub-criteria that combine to make up the criterion, with each sub-criterion occupying a double-page spread, containing the definitions of the criterion and sub-criterion, plus a list of activities within an organisation that the particular sub-criterion could be applied to.

For each sub-criterion there are three examples to illustrate how it is put into practice in three different types of organisation – a large private sector company, a large public sector organisation and a small-to-medium business, or a division of a large private sector organisation. The logo at the top of the box cross-references to that in Appendix 1 to indicate which of these three sectors the example is from.

The lower 3 boxes for each sub-criterion contain key learning points and reasons why the example above it has been included.

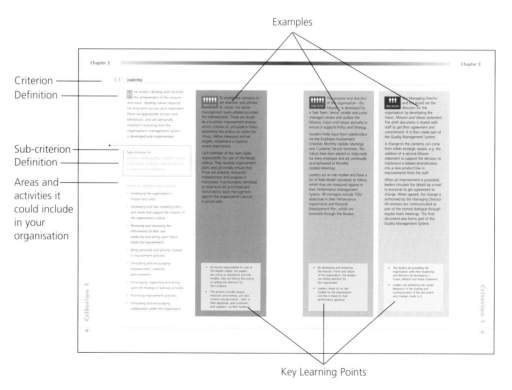

Examples

Criterion Definition

Sub-criterion Definition

Areas and activities it could include in your organisation

Key Learning Points

2.1 | Introduction

This chapter shows how the examples in this book, together with other sources of information, can help you implement improvement in your organisation. Space does not allow a comprehensive description of all improvement approaches, but there is enough detail in this chapter to get you started.

It begins by describing a simple change process that you may use. This has four key steps, based around the RADAR® (Results, Approach, Deployment, Assessment and Review) approach that underpins the philosophy of Excellence, described in Chapter 1.

A key feature of the approach is that it focuses on the results that you want to achieve. It makes use of the linkages within the Model and refers to the examples in Chapter 3 as a source of ideas for improvement action.

In addition to referring to the examples, this chapter also includes other approaches that you may wish to consider, including some widely used and well-recognised tools and techniques. This should further assist you in the implementation of improvements, as the examples provide ideas and aid communication of the benefits of using the Excellence Model.

2.2 | A Simple Change Process Using RADAR®

2.2.1 Introduction

RADAR®, described in Chapter 1, is based on the widely known 'Plan-Do-Check-Act' continuous improvement cycle that some organisations have been following since the 1950s.

The concept is to:

Plan what you need to do to achieve your goals.

Do the action/activity.

Check or review that the action/activity was successful.

Act on the results of the review, for example, by taking additional actions if you were not completely successful.

The improvement approach described below, and shown in Figure 2.1, follows similar lines.

1. Consider where there is a need for improvement based on the **results** your organisation aims to achieve. These may concern People, Customers, Partners, Society and Key Performance results. These main stakeholders were discussed in the introduction.

2. Decide what **approaches** need to be implemented or improved in order to achieve your aims. Things are never simple and there is always a variety of options that you may take. A key part of this step is to select the action to be taken.

3. **Deploy** the approaches at an appropriate level in the organisation. This is often more than just communicating

the change and usually involves a change to procedures and behaviours. Change has also to be introduced in a managed way that is culturally acceptable to increase the chances of success.

4. **Assess** and **review** the benefit of the change to ensure that the approaches have been effective. The success of this stage will depend on how well the change was planned and managed.

Figure 2.1 – The Improvement Approach.

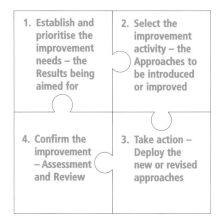

2.2.2   **Step 1: Establish and prioritise the improvement needs – the Results being aimed for**

Whoever gave the advice 'State destination before boarding train' must have had experience of racing off to take action before understanding exactly what the purpose of the action was.

Another trap is to plan to take too much action, which often leads to no action being taken at all. All organisations have limited resources, be these financial and/or human, etc. Therefore it is important to choose to take action where there is going to be the greatest payback against the chosen objectives.

Even if you think you know what needs to be done this is often based on perception and not fact. The first stage of the improvement process, therefore, is to analyse the current situation and clearly state your aims.

Many methods may be used for this analysis. Organisations that are familiar with the Excellence Model may already be practising 'self-assessment' leading to an abundance of improvement opportunities.

Additionally, you can get an insight from other activities. As part of an organisation's strategic planning activities it may perform regular SWOT analyses that include a review of the organisation's current strengths and weakness as well as a check on the opportunities and threats. Another source could be specific feedback from a stakeholder, such as a customer, or from the results of a benchmarking exercise.

When discussing analysis a key message is that 'you get what you pay for'. An organisation that seeks detailed data on which to make decisions is likely to make better decisions than one that makes decisions just on perceptions or, as is often the case, 'gut feel'. Care should be taken to avoid 'analysis paralysis', however, as things can be taken too far.

Despite these concerns it is important to choose an approach for the analysis that suits the situation. There are many ways of conducting self-assessments against the Excellence Model, including such diverse techniques as a group of managers sitting in a room for a couple of hours to get their view on where they perceive there are gaps, or conducting an 'award' style self-assessment lasting several months that involves collecting lots of data. Both methods are suitable in different situations depending on the purpose of the exercise, which can also be diverse. More detailed explanations of the methods of self-assessment are available from The British Quality Foundation in the publication *Assessing for Excellence.*

The analysis, whichever way it is done, should lead to the point where you may answer several questions. Every organisation will have their own set of questions, but they are likely to include the following:

1. What are the most important over-riding issues that the organisation has to address?

2. Which stakeholders are these issues affecting in a positive way?

3. Are there any stakeholders who will lose out?

4. What is the current performance in this area?

5. By how much must current performance improve to meet targets?

6. What will it take in terms of resource to achieve this level of performance, and can the organisation afford it?

From this list of questions it should be possible to select the priority actions. It should also be possible to screen out any improvements that are outside the organisation's current capabilities, be these market requirements, financial resource requirements, human resource availability or skill availability.

2.2.3 Step 2: Select the improvement activity – the Approaches to be introduced or improved

a. Introduction

It is vital that senior people are on board at this stage, to ensure you have their support for all future actions, as any improvement activities are more likely to occur and be successful if the leaders support them. Therefore, ensure you communicate with your senior people and educate them at all stages of the improvement process.

Rarely is it possible to say 'Yes, that's the action we must take'. In business things are complicated and there are several options that may be followed.

From all the alternatives, it is necessary to choose an option that best suits the results required. This objective should be positive and SMART (Specific, Measurable, Achievable, Realistic and Timely). The following activities may help:

1. Generate options of improvement actions that could be taken.

2. Select the option that describes what is actually going to be done.

3. Define the actual approach or approaches that are to be introduced or improved.

At this stage no consideration is given to how the implementation of the action will be managed, as this is the focus of the next step. You simply concentrate on what needs to be done to achieve the performance that was defined in the first step in terms of the approaches that have to be introduced or improved.

b. **Option generation – what could be done?**

So far all you have is an objective to improve the organisation's performance, but do not know how this will be achieved. Here you can turn to the Excellence Model to generate some options detailing what could be done to reach the required level of performance. However, first you need to understand a bit more about the Excellence Model.

Figure 2.2 – A Basic Form of the Excellence Model.

People manage the organisation's processes that deliver the level of performance. It follows that, if the performance is not at the level required, you can look at either the processes, the way that people are being managed and developed, or a combination of both to find opportunities for improvement. Understanding these linkages turns the Excellence Model into a powerful diagnostic tool.

As you saw in Chapter 1, the full Excellence Model is a little more complicated, but the principles remain the same. The elements show how the drive for Excellence is measured and supported.

The enabler criteria of the Excellence Model are concerned with how the organisation approaches Excellence:

- Leadership – how behaviours/actions support a culture of Excellence.

- Policy and Strategy – how policy and strategy are deployed into plans/actions.

- People – how the organisation releases the potential of its people.

- Partnerships and Resources – how the organisation manages resources effectively/efficiently.

- Processes – how the organisation manages and improves its processes.

The results criteria of the Excellence Model are concerned with what the organisation has achieved and is achieving:

- Customer Results – what is the customer's perception of your organisation and what are your performance indicators in this area?

- People Results – what is the staff's perception of your organisation and what are your performance indicators on this subject?

- Society Results – how does society perceive your organisation and what are your performance indicators on this subject?

- Key Performance Results – what is the organisation achieving in relation to its planned performance?

Table 2.1 – Excellence Model Details.

Criterion	Sub-criteria
1. Leadership How leaders develop and facilitate the achievement of the mission and vision, develop values required for long-term success and implement these via appropriate actions and behaviours, and are personally involved in ensuring the organisation's management system is developed and implemented.	A Leaders develop the mission, vision and values, and are role models of a culture of excellence. B Leaders are personally involved in ensuring the organisation's management system is developed, implemented and continuously improved. C Leaders are involved with customers, partners and representatives of society. D Leaders motivate, support and recognise the organisation's people.
2. Policy and Strategy How the organisation implements its mission and vision via a clear stakeholder-focused strategy, supported by relevant policies, plans, objectives, targets and processes.	A Policy and Strategy are based on the present and future needs and expectations of stakeholders. B Policy and Strategy are based on information from performance measurement, research, learning and creativity related activities. C Policy and Strategy are developed, reviewed and updated. D Policy and Strategy are deployed through a framework of key processes. E Policy and Strategy are communicated and implemented.
3. People How the organisation manages, develops and releases the full potential of its people at an individual, team-based and organisation-wide level, and plans these activities in order to support its policy and strategy and the effective operation of its processes.	A People resources are planned, managed and improved. B People's knowledge and competencies are identified, developed and sustained. C People are involved and empowered. D People and the organisation have a dialogue. E People are rewarded, recognised and cared for.
4. Partnerships and Resources How the organisation plans and manages its external partnerships and internal resources in order to support its policy and strategy and the effective operation of its processes.	A External partnerships are managed. B Finances are managed. C Buildings, equipment and materials are managed. D Technology is managed. E Information and knowledge are managed.
5. Processes How the organisation designs, manages and improves its processes in order to support its policy and strategy and fully satisfy, and generate increasing value for, its customers and other stakeholders.	A Processes are systematically designed and managed. B Processes are improved, as needed, using innovation in order to fully satisfy and generate increasing value for customers and other stakeholders. C Products and services are designed and developed based on customer needs and expectations. D Products and services are produced, delivered and serviced. E Customer relationships are managed and enhanced.

Table 2.1 – Excellence Model Details (continued).

Criterion	Sub-criteria
6. Customer Results What the organisation is achieving in relation to its external customers.	A Perception measures: overall image, products and services, sales and after-sales support, loyalty. B Performance indicators: overall image, products and services, sales and after-sales support, loyalty.
7. People Results What the organisation is achieving in relation to its people.	A Perception measures: motivation, satisfaction. B Performance indicators: achievements, motivation and involvement, satisfaction, services provided to the organisation's people.
8. Society Results What the organisation is achieving in relation to local, national and international society as appropriate.	A Perception measures: performance as a responsible citizen, involvement in the communities where it operates, activities to reduce and prevent nuisance and harm from its operations and/or throughout the life cycle of its products, reporting on activities to assist in the preservation and sustainability of resources. B Performance indicators: handling changes in employment levels, press coverage, dealings with authorities, accolades and awards received.
9. Key Performance Results What the organisation is achieving in relation to its planned performance.	A Key performance outcomes (lag): financial (share price, dividends, gross margin, net profit, sales, meeting of budgets) and non-financial (market share, time to market, volumes, success rates). B Key performance indicators (lead): processes, external resources including partnerships, financial, buildings, equipment and materials, technology, information and knowledge.

The full power of the Excellence Model is realised from the linkages between results and enablers.

Figure 2.3 – The Excellence Model – Starting with Results.

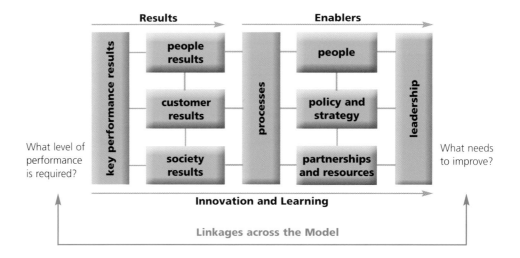

An understanding of the linkages across the Model allows you to identify potential areas for improvement. These linkages may be found at two levels:

1. Across the Model itself between results and enablers, e.g. if there is a need to improve the People Results the key question is where to look for the approaches that could be improved. Figures 2.4–2.7 illustrate these key linkages (based on the work of Diane Dibley, Information Technology Services Agency, DSS).

2. The second level of linkages is within each criterion, e.g. for Policy and Strategy the sub-criteria follow a logical sequence, and identifying which part of the chain may be weak leads to ideas for improvement. The technical description for each sub-criterion has been given in Table 2.1. Figures 2.8–2.12 detail the linkages between sub-criteria within criteria, and within the set of enablers, using everyday language. There is one figure for each of the five enablers of the Excellence Model.

Figure 2.4 – Linkages between Customer Results and Enablers.

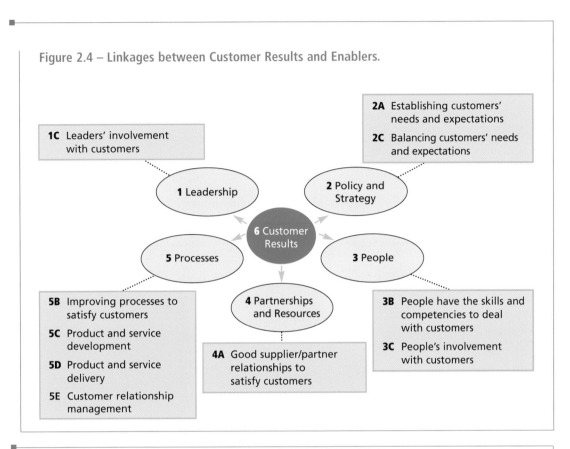

Figure 2.5 – Linkages between People Results and Enablers.

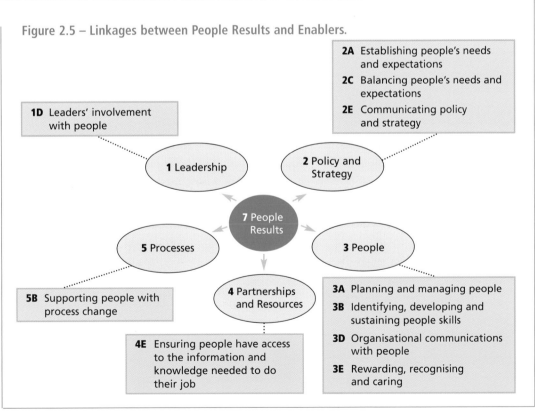

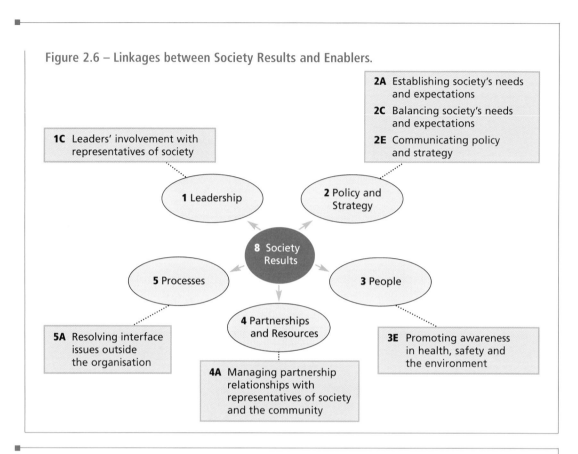

Figure 2.6 – Linkages between Society Results and Enablers.

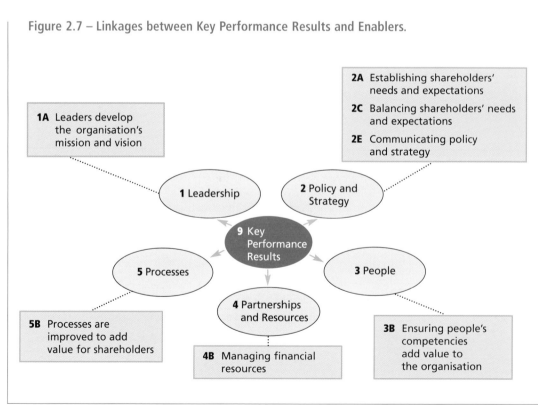

Figure 2.7 – Linkages between Key Performance Results and Enablers.

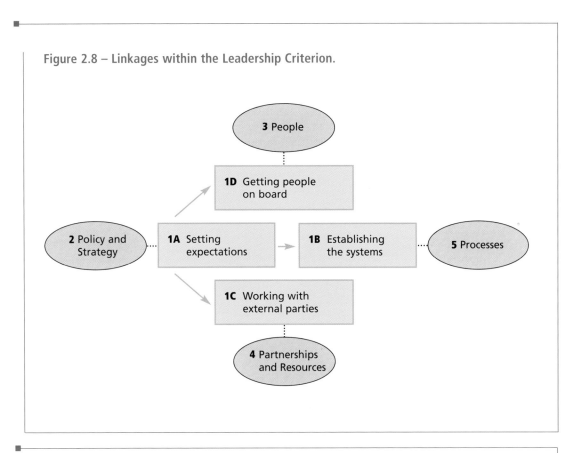

Figure 2.8 – Linkages within the Leadership Criterion.

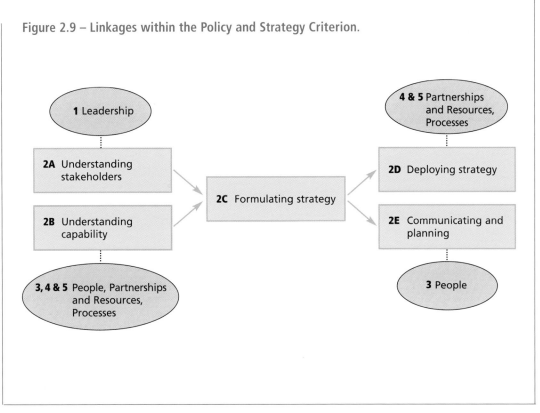

Figure 2.9 – Linkages within the Policy and Strategy Criterion.

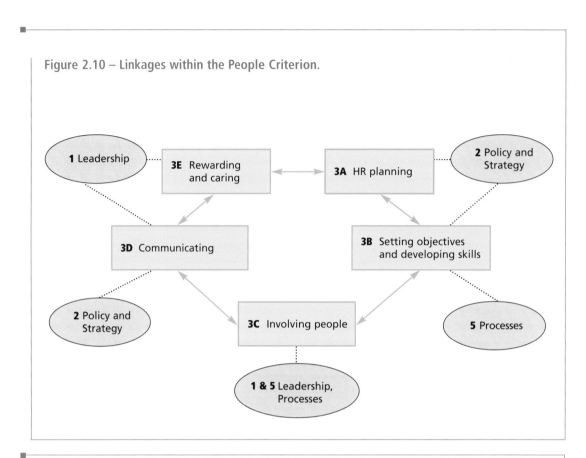

Figure 2.10 – Linkages within the People Criterion.

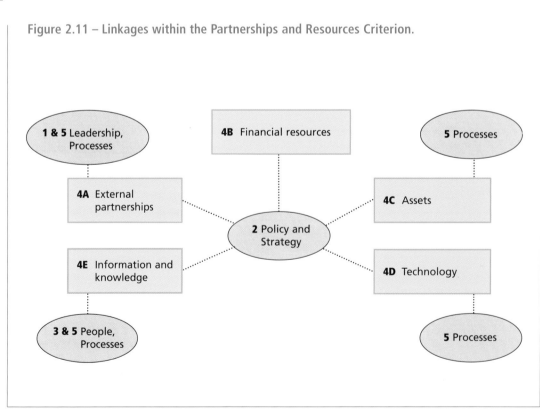

Figure 2.11 – Linkages within the Partnerships and Resources Criterion.

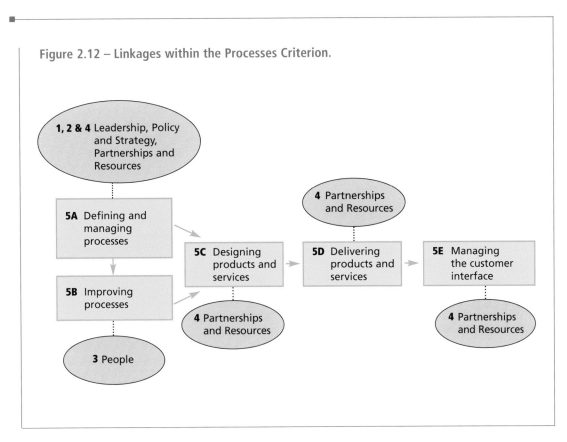

Figure 2.12 – Linkages within the Processes Criterion.

If you want to increase customer satisfaction, you may have identified that your staff are not customer focused, and further investigation may reveal that this is not an issue that training alone will solve. Part of the cause may be the lack of direction or perhaps an inappropriate strategy. The key point here is that you want to open up as many opportunities as possible before deciding what to do.

The reason why these linkages have been presented is as an aid to identifying potential options for improvement action. To use this information it is suggested that you use the following guidance:

1. First review the output from Step 1, where you identified the performance level you are seeking to obtain for a particular stakeholder grouping.

2. Next review Figures 2.4–2.7 by stakeholder grouping to identify sub-criteria that could be targeted for improvement activity.

3. Studying the five enabler figures widens your search for potential improvements by seeing what linkages there are between the particular sub-criterion and linking criteria.

4. Reference to the examples in Chapter 3 will help you understand the detail of each sub-criterion and give you additional ideas.

For example, if your organisation's objective is to increase its performance in customer satisfaction levels from 85 to 90%, refer to Figure 2.4 for Customer Results. This shows the linkages to certain enabler sub-criteria identifying possible areas for you to target for improvement, e.g. it links to 1C – Leaders' involvement with customers. Chapter 3 gives real-life examples of practices that have been carried out under this sub-criterion, and they may either be directly applicable to your organisation or lead to ideas for alternatives.

By the end of your search, you should have many potential areas for improvement activity. The next task in the process is to screen the options so that the most appropriate improvement action may be taken, i.e. prioritise.

c. **Option selection – what are you going to do?**
It is unlikely that there will be only one option as there is always the 'Do nothing' option that should be considered. It is more likely that by this point you will have a short-list of the actions that you could take. It is therefore useful to have simple tools for selecting the chosen action. When taking improvement action there is a cost, in terms of people and money, and a benefit. It is normal that the higher the cost the greater the benefit. However, this is not always the case as simple things can be extremely effective and, if inappropriate action is chosen, no matter how much effort goes into implementation, the desired performance will not be achieved.

There are several ways to prioritise improvement activities, the detail of which is outside the scope of this book. However, an important point to note at this stage is that if your organisation focuses only on one thing, such as attaining ISO 9000 certification, or gaining Investors in People, there is a chance that something could be missed.

d. **Option design – exactly what needs to be done?**
Working through the previous sections will lead you to a decision on what improvement action you should take. Now is the time to put some more detail on the idea in preparation for implementation in the next step. For example, it may have been decided to introduce an appraisal system, but the question 'How will this work in practice?' has yet to be answered. Process thinking, which is at the heart of the Excellence Model®, provides the way forward to achieve this.

Capturing the new or revised approach as a process ensures that all aspects of the improvement can be covered and communicated effectively. In defining the approach the following areas should be covered:

1. What is the aim of the process?

2. What is the scope of the new or revised process?

3. Where does the activity start and where does it end?

4. What controls need to be in place to manage the process?

5. Who will operate the approach?

6. What is their required skill and experience level?

7. What equipment and facilities are required?

8. What are the process steps?

9. What measures will be used to monitor the performance of the process?

Use of process mapping and flowcharting is a good way to document the approach and it facilitates communication.

The technique chosen may be based on a widely used approach. Therefore, to help with your improvement planning, Table 2.2 (overleaf) contains a list of some of these approaches, together with a brief description, where they have most impact in the Excellence Model and where to go for more information.

Table 2.2 – Commonly Used Approaches.

Approach	Brief Description	Where it has an impact ◄— Enabler —►						Where to go for more information
		1	2	3	4	5	Results	
Activity Based Costing (ABC)	ABC is an approach for assigning overheads to products based on *the way that costs are incurred.* It involves establishing cost pools and cost drivers. The main benefit from the approach is more informed decision-making, but a major concern is the amount of effort required to collect the data on which to base the decisions.				•			Cokins, G., *Activity-Based Cost Management Making It Work: A Manager's Guide to Implementing and Sustaining an Effective ABC System,* Irwin Professional Publications, 1996.
Annual Appraisals and Development Planning	Usually the responsibility of the immediate manager, the approach is used to review past performance targets and translate current year process goals into individual objectives and agree action plans. The approach frequently includes identifying training and development needs. In some approaches, the result of the appraisal is linked to an employee's pay.			•				Knowdell, R.L., *Building a Career Development Program: Nine Steps for Effective Implementation,* Consulting Psychologists Press, 1996.
Balanced Scorecard	First developed by Kaplan and Norton, it recognises the limitations of purely financial measurement of an organisation, which is normally short-term measurement. A scorecard has several measurement perspectives, with the original scorecard having financial, customer, internal business, innovation and learning perspectives. Balanced scorecards are normally a key output from the strategy formulation process.		•					BQF Workshop 04 – *Linking the Business Excellence Model with the Balanced Scorecard.* Kaplan, R.S. and Norton,D.P., *The Balanced Scorecard: Translating Strategy into Action,* Harvard Business School Press, Boston, MA (USA), 1996. Olve, N.G., et al., *Performance Drivers: A Practical Guide to Using the Balanced Scorecard,* John Wiley and Sons, 1999.
Best Practice Benchmarking	The continuous, systematic search for, and implementation of, best practices that lead to superior performance; it involves comparing performance with leading achievers.	•	•	•	•	•		American Productivity and Quality Center (APQC). BQF Workshop 08 – *World Class Improvement for Senior Management.*

Table 2.2 – Commonly Used Approaches (continued).

Approach	Brief Description	Where it has an impact ← Enabler →						Where to go for more information
		1	2	3	4	5	Results	
								British Quality Foundation (BQF) and European Centre for Business Excellence (EC for BE), *The X-Factor – Winning Performance Through Business Excellence*, London, 1999. MacDonald, J. and Tanner, S., *Understanding Benchmarking in a Week,* Hodder and Stoughton, 1996. O'Dell, C.S., et al., *If Only We Knew What We Know: The Transfer of Internal Knowledge and Best Practice,* Free Press, 1998.
Business Process Re-engineering (BPR)	The fundamental re-think and re-design of a business process, its structure and associated management systems to deliver major or step improvements in performance.					•		Hunt, V.D. and Hunt, D.V., *Process Mapping: How to Re-engineer Your Business Processes,* John Wiley and Sons, 1996. Miller, L.C.E., *Business Process Re-engineering: A Management Guidebook* (2nd Edition), Vertical Systems, Inc., 1996.
Charter Mark Framework	Government award scheme for recognising and encouraging excellence in public service. It concentrates on results – the service the customer actually receives, putting the users first, and delivering a first-class service.					•	•	Publications and leaflets, e.g. *Charter Mark, Guide for Applicants and Why You Should Apply*, are available from the Charter Unit Publications Line on 0845 722 3242.
Communication Strategies	As part of the organisation's overall policy and strategy, clearly defined guidelines for ensuring effective vertical and horizontal communications in all media, both within the organisation and externally. It is reviewed, updated and improved periodically, based on feedback from stakeholders.	•	•	•	•	•		Hodgdon, L.A., *Visual Strategies for Improving Communication,* Quirk Roberts Publishing,1995.

Table 2.2 – Commonly Used Approaches (continued).

Approach	Brief Description	Where it has an impact ← Enabler →					Results	Where to go for more information
		1	2	3	4	5	Results	
Competitive Benchmarking	The identification of external comparison data such that an organisation's performance relative to its competitors may be determined.		•			•	•	Bendell, T., et al., *Benchmarking for Competitive Advantage* (2nd Edition), Financial Times Management, 1997. Boxwell R.J., Jr., *Benchmarking for Competitive Advantage*, McGraw-Hill, 1993. Camp, R.C., *Business Process Benchmarking; finding and implementing best practice*, ASQC Quality Press, Milwaukee, WI (USA), 1995.
Cost of Quality Measurement	The concept was introduced to focus senior management attention on the cost of quality problems. In doing this it promoted the need for quality in a language they could understand. Two factors are normally considered – the cost of non-conformance, e.g. the cost of the rectification of defects or scrap and a cost associated with lost business, and the cost of quality, which covers the cost of all the activities that aim to prevent a quality failure. These include prevention, appraisal and training costs.					•	•	Dale, B.G. and Plunkett, J.J., *Quality Costings*, Chapman and Hall, London, 1991. Hronec, S.M., *Vital Signs: Using Quality, Time and Cost Performance Measurements to Chart Your Company's Future*, Amacom, 1993. Payson, S., *Quality Measurement in Economics: New Perspectives on the Evolution of Goods and Services*, Edward Elgar Publications, 1994
Deming's Plan-Do-Check-Act Cycle	Deming's cycle of continuous improvement – Plan-Do-Check-Act.		•					Deming, W.E., *Out of the Crisis*, MIT, Cambridge, Mass., (USA), 1982. Walton, M. and Deming, W.E., *Deming Management Method*, Perigee, 1998.

Table 2.2 – Commonly Used Approaches (continued).

Approach	Brief Description	Where it has an impact ◄— Enabler —►						Where to go for more information
		1	2	3	4	5	Results	
Employee Surveys	These are used to gather information from employees about their needs, expectations and satisfaction. There are many ways to collect the information, including: focus groups, questionnaires, workshops, interviews, telephone and e-mail. The results should be analysed, publicised and responded to.		•	•			•	Folkman, J. and Zenger, J., *Employee Surveys That Make A Difference: Using Customised Feedback Tools to Transform Your Organisation,* Executive Excellence, 1999. Kraut, A.I., and Kraut, A J, *Organisational Surveys: Tools for Assessment and Change (Social and Behavioural Science)* Jossey-Bass, 1996.
Failure Mode, Effect and Criticality Analysis (FMECA)	Processes can be analysed to determine possible modes of failure and their effects on the performance of the product or operation. FMECA is the study of potential failures to determine their effects, with results ranked in order of seriousness.				•			Dorner, D., et al., *The Logic of Failure: Recognising and Avoiding Error in Complex Situations,* Perseus Press, 1997. Stamatis, D.H., *Failure Mode and Effect Analysis: FMEA from Theory to Execution,* AMER Society for Quality, 1995.
Flowcharting	A graphical method used to record the detail of processes by showing them as a series of tasks and activities using standard symbols. Use is normally made of software to draw the diagrams.				•			Boillot, M.H., et al., *Essentials of Flowcharting,* WCB/McGraw-Hill, 1995.
HASAW	The Health and Safety at Work Act (HASAW) seeks to secure the health, safety and welfare of persons at work, for protecting others against risks to health or safety in connection with the activities of persons at work, for controlling the keeping and use and preventing the unlawful acquisition, possession and use of dangerous substances, and for controlling certain emissions to the atmosphere.			•	•			Diberardinis, L.J., *Handbook of Occupational Safety and Health,* John Wiley and Sons, 1998. Woodside, G., *Environmental, Health and Safety Portable Handbook,* McGraw-Hill, 1998.

Table 2.2 – Commonly Used Approaches (continued).

Approach	Brief Description	Where it has an impact ◄— Enabler —►						Where to go for more information
		1	2	3	4	5	Results	
IDEFO (Integration Definition Function Modelling)	A structured graphical framework for describing and improving business processes based on an approach developed by the American armed forces. A model consists of a hierarchical series of diagrams, text and glossary, cross-referenced through boxes (process components) and arrows (data and objects).					•		Barker, R. and Longman, C., *Case Method: Function and Process Modelling*, Addison-Wesley Publishing Company, 1992. De Carteret, C. and Vidgen, R., *Data Modelling for Information Systems*, Financial Times Management, 1995.
Investors in People (IIP)	A UK National Standard that sets a level of good practice for training and development of people to achieve business goals. The Investors in People certificate is awarded to organisations that pass an external assessment.		•					Gilliland, N., *Developing Your Business Through Investors in People*, Gower Publishing Company, 1997.
ISO 9000 Based Quality Management Systems	It sets out how the methods incorporating all the activities associated with quality in an organisation are implemented to ensure that the performance requirements and needs of the customer are fully met.			•	•	•		British Standards Institution: *ISO/CDI 9001:2000 Quality Management Systems*. Hoyle, D., *ISO9000 Pocket Guide*, Butterworth-Heinemann, 1998. Rothery, B., *ISO9000*, Gower Publications Company.
ISO 14000	A specification for environmental management systems for ensuring and demonstrating compliance *with stated policies and objectives*. It can enable any organisation to establish an effective management system as a foundation for sound environmental performance and participation in environmental auditing schemes. It is now possible to undergo a third party audit and receive a certificate of compliance.				•	•		British Standards Institution. Block, M.R. and Marash, I.R., *Integrating ISO4001 into a Quality Management System*, AMER Society for Quality, 2000. Tanner, D. and Bellamy, R., *Environmental Management in Asia: A Guide to ISO14000*, AET Limited, 1997.

Table 2.2 – Commonly Used Approaches (continued).

| Approach | Brief Description | Where it has an impact | | | | | | Where to go for more information |
| | | ←— Enabler —→ | | | | | Results | |
		1	2	3	4	5		
JIT (Just-in-Time)	Concerns the delivery of materials to manufacturing locations at the point that they are required for production. The emphasis is on increased efficiency and reduction in waste, shortening of lead times, improvement in quality, continuous improvement and simplicity.				•	•		Hirano, H. and Hiroyuki, H., *JIT Factory Revolution: A Pictorial Guide to Factory Design of the Future*, Productivity Press, 1989. Petroff, J.N., *Handbook of MRP III/JIT Integration and Implementation*, Prentice Hall, 1993.
Job Descriptions	Used to define the requirements of a specific job and as a reference for recruitment. They should contain, as a minimum, activities to be undertaken in performing the job and requirements of the individual in terms of experience, skills and training.			•				Plachy, R.J., *Results Orientated Job Descriptions: More Than 225 Models to Use or Adapt – With Guidelines for Creating Your Own*, Amacom, 1993. Plachy, S.J. and Plachy, R.J., *More Results – Orientated Job Descriptions: 226 Models to Use or Adapt – With Guidelines for Creating Your Own*, Amacom, 1998.
Leadership Assessment and 360° Appraisal	Assessment of a leader's performance against established leadership criteria. Data is normally collected through surveying a leader's superiors, peers and direct staff.	•		•				Edwards, M.R. and Ewen, A.J. (Contributor), *360 Degree Feedback: The Powerful New Model for Employee Assessment and Performance Improvement*, Amacom, 1996. Humphrey, B. and Stokes, J., *The 21st Century Supervisor: Self Assessment – Nine Essential Skills for Developing Frontline Leaders*, Jossey-Bass, 1999.

Table 2.2 – Commonly Used Approaches (continued).

Approach	Brief Description	Where it has an impact ◄— Enabler —►						Where to go for more information
		1	2	3	4	5	Results	
Market Surveys and Customer Observations	These are used to acquire information about customer needs and expectations, which informs policy and strategy and is used as a basis for product and service development. There are several types and the right mix is essential to ensure the correct information is gathered.		•			•		Jarboe, G.R., *The Marketing Research Project Manual,* West Wadsworth, 1996. Wing, M.J., et al., *The Arthur Andersen Guide to Talking With Your Customers: What They Will Tell You About Your Business: When You Ask the Right Questions,* Upstart Publishing Company, 1977.
Materials Materials Requirement Planning II (MRP II)	Requirement Planning is a set of techniques that uses bill of materials, inventory on hand and on order, and the production schedule or plan to calculate the quantities and timing of materials. MRPII is a computer-based system that arose from an appreciation of the need to time and phase materials with resource availability so as to achieve a given output date.				•	•		Oden, H.W., et al., *Handbook of Material* and *Capacity Requirements Planning,* McGraw-Hill, 1993. Orlicky, J. and Plossl, G.W., *Orlicky's Material Requirements Planning,* McGraw-Hill, 1994.
Policy Deployment (or Goal Translation) Process	This identifies how to achieve the mission, i.e. translate the 'what's' into 'how's', right through the organisation.	•	•					Alai, Y., *Hoshin Kanri: Policy Deployment for Successful TQM,* Productivity Press, 1991. Sheridan, B.M., *Policy Deployment: The TQM Approach to Long-Range Planning,* AMER, Society for Quality, 1993.
Political, Economic, Social, Technology, Legal, Environmental (PESTLE) Analysis	Identifying and understanding political, economic, demographic, social, technological, legal and environmental issues and their effect on the organisation's policy and strategy.		•					Johnson, G. and Scholes, K., *Exploring Corporate Strategy* (5th Edition), Prentice Hall Europe, 1999.

Table 2.2 – Commonly Used Approaches (continued).

| Approach | Brief Description | Where it has an impact ← Enabler → | | | | | | Where to go for more information |
		1	2	3	4	5	Results	
Prioritisation of Improvement	The use of simple tools to assist in the prioritisation of defined improvement opportunities, taking into account the level of benefit and the amount of effort required. The ideal improvement activity will have a high impact on the organisation for a low investment in resource, financial investment or need to overcome resistance.					•		Oakland, J.S., *Total Organisational Excellence – Achieving World Class Performance*, (1st Edition), Butterworth-Heinmann, 1999. Oakland, J.S., *Total Quality Management – The Route to Improving Performance* (2nd Edition), Butterworth-Heinmann, 1993.
Process Mapping/Modelling	Using simple flowcharts or more advanced techniques such as IDEF0 to describe what a process does, what it controls, what things it works on, what means it uses to perform its functions and what it produces. Process modelling involves the creation of 'What if' scenarios as a part of improvement activities such as Business Process Re-engineering (BPR).					•		Damelio, R., *The Basics of Process Mapping*, Productivity Inc., 1996. Hunt, V.D., and Hunt, D.V., *Process Mapping: How to Re-engineer Your Business Processes*, John Wiley and Sons, 1996. Scholz-Reiter, B. and Stickel, E., *Business Process Modelling*, Springer Verlag, 1996.
Project Management	There are many approaches to managing projects but they all involve balancing the scope of the change (how much is achieved) and quality of the change (how well it is achieved) against how much it costs and how long it takes. Project management includes a variety of tools and techniques such as Project Definitions, Project Plans and Gantt Charts.					•		Cleland, D.I. and King, W.R., *Project Management Handbook*, John Wiley and Sons, 1988. Turner, J.R., *The Handbook of Project-Based Management*, McGraw-Hill, 1993.

Table 2.2 – Commonly Used Approaches (continued).

Approach	Brief Description	Where it has an impact Enabler						Where to go for more information
		1	2	3	4	5	Results	
Psychometric Tests	Methods to assess an individual's behaviour and preferences by getting them to complete a questionnaire where they have to rate a series of statements. Two of the better-known tests are FIRO-B (Fundamental Interpersonal Relationship Orientation Behaviour) Instrument and the Myers-Briggs Type Indicator. The first looks at the dynamics of relationships and the second is a tool for team development.	•		•				Nunnally, J.C. and Bernstein, I.H., *Psychometric Theory* (McGraw-Hill Series in Social Psychology), McGraw-Hill College Division, 1994. Parkinson, M., *How to Master Psychometric Tests: Winning Strategies for Test Takers,* Kogan Page Ltd, 1998.
Quality Function Deployment (QFD)	A technique to compare the technical or operating characteristics of a product or service with customer needs. A multi-disciplinary team carries it out.				•			Cohen, L. and Cohen, L., *Quality Function Deployment: How to Make QFD Work for You (Engineering Process Improvement),* Addison-Wesley Publications Company, 1995. Revelle, J.B., et al., *The QFD Handbook,* John Wiley and Sons, 1998.
Six Sigma	The number of standard deviations from the average setting of a process to the tolerance limit. In statistical terms, this translates to 3.4 defects per million. 'Six Sigma' has become an approach to managing the output of manufacturing operations to ensure high levels of quality.				•			BQF Workshop 09 – *Six Sigma and the Business Excellence Model.* Breyfogle, F.W., *Implementing Six Sigma: Smarter Solutions Using Statistical Methods,* John Wiley and Sons, 1999. Harry, M.J. and Schrodeder, R., *Six Sigma: The Breakthrough Management Strategy Revolutionising The World's Top Corporations,* Doubleday, 1999.

Table 2.2 – Commonly Used Approaches (continued).

Approach	Brief Description	Where it has an impact ← Enabler →						Where to go for more information
		1	2	3	4	5	Results	
Stakeholder Analysis	A way of analysing which stakeholders need to be managed when trying to manage change. Stakeholders, who can be internal or external, have a level of interest and a degree of power, e.g. stakeholders with high levels of interest in any change and who possess high levels of power need to be carefully managed. Other stakeholders may only need to be kept informed.		•	•		•		Johnson, G. and Scholes, K., *Exploring Corporate Strategy* (5th Edition), Prentice Hall Europe, 1999.
Statistical Process Control (SPC)	Measurement of the output of a process at regular intervals. A simple mathematical calculation allows the determination of the quality level of the output. When plotted on a 'Control Chart', it is possible to differentiate the expected 'normal causes' of variation from 'special causes' of variation, which signal a problem with the process. The Control Chart also allows the process to be monitored over time and thereby the forecasting of future potential quality problems.					•		Abbott, J.C., *Practical Understanding of Capability by Implementing Statistical Process Control*, SPC (3rd Edition), Robert Houston Smith Publisher, 1999. Oakland, J.S., *Statistical Process Control: A Practical Guide* (4th Edition), Butterworth-Heinemann, 1999. Quesenberry, C.P., *SPC Methods for Quality Improvement*, John Wiley and Sons,1997.
Strengths, Weaknesses, Opportunities, Threats (SWOT) Analysis	A method for identifying current strengths and weaknesses within the organisation and future potential opportunities and threats.		•					Johnson, G. and Scholes, K, *Exploring Corporate Strategy* (5th Edition), Prentice Hall Europe, 1999.
Suggestion Schemes	A method for employees to propose ideas for improvement within the organisation by a number of routes, sometimes anonymously, using boxes placed around the workplace, or via their line manager, either informally or formally. The management considers all suggestions and responses are publicised.			•		•		Martin, C.L., and Bassford, R., (Contributor), *Employee Suggestion Systems: Boosting Productivity and Profits (Fifty-MinuteSeries)*, Crisp Publishing, 1997.

Table 2.2 – Commonly Used Approaches (continued).

Approach	Brief Description	Where it has an impact ←— Enabler —→						Where to go for more information
		1	2	3	4	5	Results	
Supplier Partnerships	The philosophy is that, through co-operation, rather than confrontation, both parties benefit. It is a longer-term view, emphasising total cost rather than product price. Long-term, stable relationships are sought rather than short-term quick advantage transactions.	•			•			Hale, R.L., *Managing Supplier Quality: How to Develop Customer-Supplier Partnerships That Work*, Monochrome Press, 1994. Stimson, *J.A., Supplier Partnerships (The Purchasing Excellence Series)*, Pt Publishing, 1999.
Total Productive Maintenance (TPM)	An approach developed in Japan to involve production workers in the maintenance of their own equipment such that manufacturing becomes more productive. Based on a 'six pillars' concept that includes training and continuous improvement as well as maintenance, the approach also has the benefit of increasing people involvement and team working.			•		•		Willmott, P., *Total Productive Maintenance: The Western Way*, Butterworth-Heinemann, 1995.
Total Quality Management (TQM)	Total Quality Management (TQM) is far wider in its application than just assuring product or service quality – it is a way of managing people and business processes to ensure complete customer satisfaction at every stage, internally and externally.	•		•	•	•		Choppin, J., *Quality Through People: A Blueprint for Proactive Total Quality Management*, Rushmere Wynne, Bedford (UK), 1997. Crampa, D.,*Total Quality – A User's Guide for Implementation*, Addison-Wesley, Reading, MA, USA, 1992. Oakland, J.S., *Total Quality Management-Text with Cases* (2nd Edition), Butterworth-Heinemann, 2000.

2.2.4 Step 3: Take action – Deploying the new or revised approaches

So far you have established what level of performance is required and what action you believe needs to be taken to deliver this level of performance. Now is the time to take the action.

It is considered good practice to define the change using a project brief or terms of reference. This document builds on the definition of the aims of the change that were developed in Step 1. For small changes these can be quite brief documents and may include entries such as:

- The aim of the change together with performance objectives/ success measures.

- Scope of the change – what is included and what is outside the improvement activity, e.g. the improvement may be only deployed in one area of the organisation or at one organisational level.

- What benefits will be delivered as a result of the change and when will they be delivered?

- What the estimated cost of the change will be and over what time-frame.

- Who will be affected by the change, in both a positive and negative sense?

Not only does the project definition provide clarity over what is to be achieved, it also acts as a reference document that may be referred back to once the change is complete. Such a document also allows changes to the project to be implemented in a controlled way.

When implementing change it is important to recognise that it is not a good idea to simply announce the change, take the action and then expect that the improved performance will be maintained. Before taking the improvement action it is essential to get people on board and to spend time explaining why the change is necessary and that it is not a one-off exercise. The change will be made to meet future objectives and it is important to point out that more change will probably follow.

It is crucial to do this with the people the change will affect. The examples contained in Chapter 3 of this book can be used to explain what other organisations are doing as a way of educating people regarding change. They may also be used to overcome barriers and to show what is possible.

Once the change has been implemented action is often necessary to make the change stick, e.g. organisations may change their reward and remuneration policies to encourage certain behaviours and to make sure that old habits do not return.

Preparing a simple project plan will be a worthwhile investment to manage the changes in a controlled way. Any change has to balance three factors:

- What is achieved – the quality of the output.

- What it costs – what resource is required.

- What time – how long it will take.

These factors are often traded against each other as an organisation seeks to implement the best solution in the shortest time possible and at minimal cost. Lengthening the timescale of a project to improve the output almost always increases the cost.

There are many tools and techniques that can be used to manage the balance of these three factors, a description of which is outside the scope of this book. Useful references for further information have been included in Table 2.2.

2.2.5   **Step 4: Confirm the improvement – Assessment and Review**

A key benefit from producing a project brief is that it provides a useful reference against which to determine the success of the improvement action. If the original aims have been achieved then the action may be closed. If not, it might be necessary to return to Step 2 and generate some more options for improvement activity.

Whatever the outcome of the assessment against the original aims, it is useful to conduct a 'Post-Completion Review' to record what has been learnt and how change may be handled more effectively in the future. Typical questions for a post-completion review include:

- Were the aims and objectives achieved?

- Did the project deliver on time?

- How did the actual cost compare with the estimated cost?

- How well was the team working?

- What went well?

- What could be improved? For example, were there any problems that could have been avoided?

- How was the project team perceived by the stakeholders in terms of how it delivered the project?

2.3 | Summary

The aim of this chapter was to present a simple approach for improving the performance of your organisation based on RADAR®. The approach includes several aspects of change management, including the need to establish clear objectives for the change, selecting the most appropriate actions and project managing the change.

The examples that follow in Chapter 3 may be used for many purposes, including as a source of information to stimulate ideas on what areas to improve. In addition, they also support the change process by using them:

- To educate people and communicate the approaches.

- To overcome barriers by demonstrating what is actually possible.

- To promote Excellence to all stakeholder groups, be these shareholders, customers, partners, society or people.

The Excellence Model

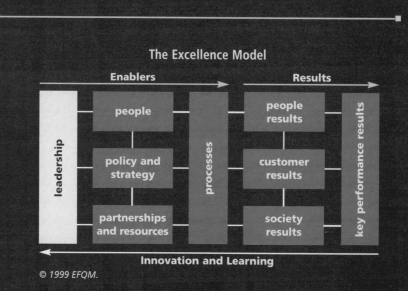

"Leaders set the organisation's direction, a plan for getting there, ensure all employees are on board and are involved with key stakeholders."

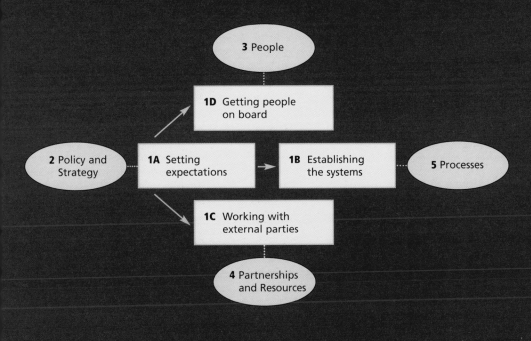

Linkages between
the sub-criteria
and with the
other enablers

3.1 Leadership

How leaders develop and facilitate the achievement of the mission and vision, develop values required for long-term success and implement these via appropriate actions and behaviours, and are personally involved in ensuring that the organisation's management system is developed and implemented.

Sub-criterion 1A:
Leaders develop the mission, vision and values and are role models of a culture of excellence.

Areas to address may include:

- *Developing the organisation's mission and vision;*

- *Developing and role modelling ethics and values that support the creation of the organisation's culture;*

- *Reviewing and improving the effectiveness of their own leadership and acting upon future leadership requirements;*

- *Being personally and actively involved in improvement activities;*

- *Stimulating and encouraging empowerment, creativity and innovation;*

- *Encouraging, supporting and acting upon the findings of learning activities;*

- *Prioritising improvement activities;*

- *Stimulating and encouraging collaboration within the organisation.*

PRIVATE SECTOR

To enable the company to set direction and achieve its Vision, the senior management team address priorities for improvement. These are driven by a business improvement process, which consists of: articulate a Vision, determine the actions to realise the Vision, define measures and set targets, then implement a rigorous review mechanism.

Each member of the team takes responsibility for one of the Model criteria. They develop improvement plans and personally ensure that these are properly resourced and implemented, and that progress is monitored. Improvements identified at local level are prioritised and resourced by local management against the organisation's annual business plan.

- By having responsibility for one of the Model criteria, the leaders are acting as champions and role models; they are linking this activity to setting the direction for the company.

- The process includes targets, measures and reviews, and also involves key personnel – staff, in their appraisals, and customers and suppliers, via their feedback.

PUBLIC SECTOR The purpose and direction of the organisation – the Mission – is developed by a Task Team. Senior, middle and junior managers review and update the Mission, Vision and Values annually to ensure it supports Policy and Strategy.

Leaders invite input from stakeholders via the Employee Involvement initiative, Monthly Update Meetings and Customer Service Seminars. The Values have been placed on help-cards for every employee and are continually re-emphasised at Monthly Update Meetings.

Leaders act as role models and have a list of Role Model Standards to follow, which they are measured against in their Performance Management System. All managers include TQM objectives in their Performance Agreements and Personal Development Plan, which are reviewed through the Review.

- By developing and reviewing the Mission, Vision and Values of the organisation, the leaders are setting direction for the organisation.

- Leaders clearly act as role models for the organisation and this is linked to their performance appraisal.

 SMALL/MEDIUM The Managing Director and the Board set the direction for the organisation by developing the Vision, Mission and Values statement. The draft document is shared with staff to get their agreement and commitment. It is then made part of the Quality Management System.

A change to the contents can come from either strategic review, e.g. the addition of a second Mission statement to support the decision to implement a related diversification into a new product line or improvements from the staff.

When an improvement is proposed, leaders circulate the details by e-mail to everyone to obtain agreement to change. When agreed, the change is authorised by the Managing Director. All revisions are communicated as part of the normal dialogue through regular team meetings. The final document also forms part of the Quality Management System.

- The leaders are providing the organisation with clear leadership and direction by developing a Vision, Mission and Value statement.

- Leaders are exhibiting role model behaviour in the sharing and communication of the document and changes made to it.

Criterion 1

3.1 Leadership

How leaders develop and facilitate the achievement of the mission and vision, develop values required for long-term success and implement these via appropriate actions and behaviours, and are personally involved in ensuring the organisation's management system is developed and implemented.

Sub-criterion 1B:
Leaders are personally involved in ensuring the organisation's management system is developed, implemented and continuously improved.

Areas to address may include:

- *Aligning the organisation's structure to support delivery of its policy and strategy;*

- *Ensuring a system for managing processes is developed and implemented;*

- *Ensuring a process for the development, deployment and updating of policy and strategy is developed and implemented;*

- *Ensuring a process for the measurement, review and improvement of key results is developed and implemented;*

- *Ensuring a process, or processes, for stimulating, identifying, planning and implementing improvements to enabling approaches, e.g. through creativity, innovation and learning activities, is developed and implemented.*

 PRIVATE SECTOR Leaders participate in a systematic quality system review process based on a model that has been developed by the organisation, and which has been refined over many years. Using a self-assessment approach, the reviews are conducted every two years.

Feedback used to be given in a formal report but, based on review, the process has been refined so that feedback is more consultative. The assessors and the business unit's management team discuss informally the outputs from the assessment. Improvement action taken as a result of the feedback is through the business unit's business planning process.

The scoring system is complex and focuses on determining action. The evidence of effectiveness is that over time business units have observed an improvement in their overall score. The approach is supported by the President's Award, which looks at the aspects of the score achieved in the reviews plus the business unit's performance.

- Leaders are personally and directly involved in the process to review and improve the organisation's management system.

- There is evidence that this has led to actions which have resulted in improvements to the business.

The top 30 leaders formed teams to look at the impact of the future Strategy of the organisation. These teams determined what the major activities would be in the future organisation. They were interviewed to determine the impact of the new activities on the existing processes. This led to a set of revised top-level process maps being produced, which were fed back to the senior team to gain acceptance.

Leaders supported and were involved in designing and implementing the organisation's management system – the Business Management System (BMS). It documents how the activities are managed, thereby deploying the policy and strategy through a process framework. A range of measures has been developed to determine the effectiveness of the BMS.

The senior team also determined the top-level policies, which are implemented through the BMS.

- Leaders are instrumental in the formation of the organisation's management system and in its implementation.

- There are measures to determine the effectiveness of the management system.

 The leaders define improvement priorities, using a well-established process based on the strategic objectives and Mission of the business, which is refined through several review cycles. They also evaluate such projects through a review process which has been developed into a systematic site-wide audit.

The cycle includes strategic and business excellence reviews, a monthly report analysing short-term performance issues, quarterly customer and supplier review meetings and weekly management meetings.

Each year the quality manager feeds the results of a self-assessment into the strategic review, and this process is also reviewed annually. Managers do most of the training and facilitating of improvement teams and/or take part in them.

- Leaders are personally involved in ensuring the organisation's management system is continuously improved.

- Leaders ensure that the process involves customers, suppliers and staff.

Criterion 1

3.1 Leadership

How leaders develop and facilitate the achievement of the mission and vision, develop values required for long-term success and implement these via appropriate actions and behaviours, and are personally involved in ensuring the organisation's management system is developed and implemented.

Sub-criterion 1C:
Leaders are involved with customers, partners and representatives of society.

Areas to address may include:

- *Meeting, understanding and responding to needs and expectations;*

- *Establishing and participating in partnerships;*

- *Establishing and participating in joint improvement activity;*

- *Recognising individuals and teams of stakeholders for their contribution to the business, for loyalty etc;*

- *Participating in professional bodies, conferences and seminars, particularly promoting and supporting Excellence;*

- *Supporting and engaging in activities that aim to improve the environment and the organisation's contribution to society.*

 PRIVATE SECTOR Leaders are involved with external organisations, including face-to-face consultation with customers. Methods of gathering information include formal consultation groups on location of retail outlets, outlet rationalisation, presenting at, or attending, meetings of key interest groups. Agreed client processes are set up for managers to develop relationships with clients to assess the company's own performance and identify opportunities for improvement.

There are joint initiatives with suppliers that are measured through a systematic assessment process.

Managers are also actively involved in the BQF and EFQM and with the business community, giving presentations, acting as external assessors, sharing management approaches, membership of the industry lobbying organisation and the Best Practice Club to share best practice.

- Leaders work closely with a wide range of external organisations including customers, suppliers and society.

- There are processes for measuring the effectiveness of customer and supplier involvement.

Regional directors have established a framework of strategic agreements with local authorities, local enterprise companies and health boards to achieve more effective targeting of resources. There are joint improvement activities with customers, e.g. the provision of private financing to social housing, the development of a self-help pack to allow associations to run customer satisfaction surveys.

Regular meetings are held with national bodies and local authorities to discuss mutual interests in developing policy and strategy. Active participation in professional bodies is encouraged and senior managers are frequently asked to speak at conferences, both nationally and internationally.

A set of customer relationship principles has been developed, and has been successful in maintaining generally high satisfaction levels.

- Leaders establish, and participate in, partnerships, joint improvement activities and professional bodies.

- Leaders support activities to improve the organisation's contribution to society.

 The company philosophy is for leaders to build relationships with external organisations, including all its customers, suppliers and outside support agencies. The business development manager meets with existing and potential customers to discuss their needs and any improvements that can be made, and also gives sales presentations to the staff of customers to ensure they are informed when dealing with their customers.

The Managing Director meets with all raw material suppliers annually to discuss mutual beneficial improvements, e.g. in partnership with a haulier, a more flexible delivery service is available for customers.

The Managing Director also lectures to management students, gives talks on quality issues, is on an Investors in People (IIP) recognition panel and is a judge for the regional quality award.

- Leaders actively participate in professional bodies, including promoting excellence and IIP.

- Leaders are involved in mutually beneficial partnership relationships with suppliers.

Criterion 1

3.1 Leadership

How leaders develop and facilitate the achievement of the mission and vision, develop values required for long-term success and implement these via appropriate actions and behaviours, and are personally involved in ensuring the organisation's management system is developed and implemented.

'Sub-criterion 1D:
Leaders motivate, support and recognise the organisation's people.

Areas to address may include:

- *Personally communicating the organisation's mission, vision, values, policy and strategy, plans objectives and targets to people;*

- *Being accessible, actively listening and responding to people;*

- *Helping and supporting people to achieve their plans, objectives and targets;*

- *Encouraging and enabling people to participate in improvement activity;*

- *Recognising both team and individual efforts, at all levels within the organisation, in a timely and appropriate manner.*

PRIVATE SECTOR

To ensure all staff are on board, a 'Your Shout' programme has been introduced where the Director visits main locations to collect feedback yearly. In addition, the company intranet system is used to communicate messages from the senior team and there is a monthly 'Voicecomm' from the Director where staff may dial a number to receive a briefing message. The system, which was introduced to meet the needs of the field engineers with no intranet access, also allows upward feedback.

Other leaders are involved with the communication process, e.g. road shows – "Talking Shop" – are held for technicians to promote ideas and understanding within field operations. A team-briefing process is used to cascade messages from the board on a monthly basis. The process includes upward feedback and details of recognition that have been given to staff for consideration by the board. It reviews the recognition and may consider giving a higher award, which are sometimes linked with the Annual Conference. Awards are presented by the Director.

- Leaders support staff and ensure they are motivated by being aware of what is happening throughout the organisation.

- Leaders also ensure that the staff have opportunities to comment and contribute.

PUBLIC SECTOR Leaders promote recognition by encouraging all staff to appreciate each others' efforts with a simple "Thank you". Within the Business Plan, there is a target of complimenting a colleague a minimum of once a week, and team leaders have found that leading by example is the only way to encourage this behaviour.

Leaders also support staff by accommodating further education requests and funding courses. These are seen as a definite reward for those wishing to pursue an external qualification.

People are encouraged to participate in improvement activity through The Performance Improvement Team (PIT) which has been tasked with impacting change within the business and agreeing best practice. Leaders have supported staff by providing training for those involved in the PITs.

- Leaders motivate people by involving them in in-house improvement activities.
- Leaders help and support staff to achieve personal goals and educational aspirations.
- The organisation's ethos is that recognition is seen to be evident at all levels.

 SMALL/MEDIUM Leaders believe in the need to promote and foster motivation based on ownership of the Mission and aims of the organisation, and a search for personal excellence. Recognition of staff efforts and achievements is a key component of the culture, and leaders ensure the achievement of appropriate qualifications are recognised by an upgrading or promotion, and take significant interest in the outcome of improvement projects, inviting participating staff to present a summary of the work at their meeting.

Staff are also actively supported and encouraged to document their achievements and submit successful projects for external recognition in national schemes, with resulting successes as both regional award winners and national finalists.

- Leaders clearly promote an open culture of reward, recognition, support and motivation for their staff.
- The outputs of this culture are used for the personal benefit of the staff, to ensure they are on board, and for the organisation at a regional level.

Criterion 1

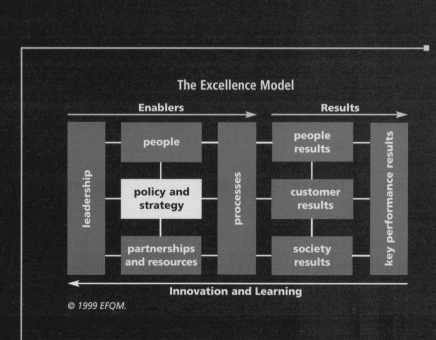

The Excellence Model

Enablers

Results

leadership

people

policy and
strategy

processes

partnerships
and resources

people
results

customer
results

society
results

key performance results

Innovation and Learning

© 1999 EFQM.

"Leaders develop a policy and strategy based on the organisation's capabilities and on stakeholders' needs, and ensure it is reviewed, updated, communicated and implemented."

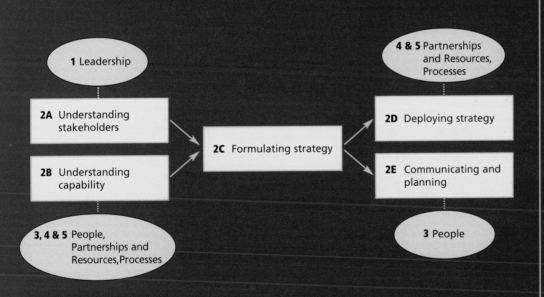

1 Leadership

4 & 5 Partnerships and Resources, Processes

2A Understanding stakeholders

2B Understanding capability

2C Formulating strategy

2D Deploying strategy

2E Communicating and planning

3, 4 & 5 People, Partnerships and Resources, Processes

3 People

Linkages between the sub-criteria and with the other enablers

3.2 | Policy and Strategy

How the organisation implements its mission and vision via a clear stakeholder-focused strategy, supported by relevant policies, plans, objectives, targets and processes.

Sub-criterion 2A:
Policy and strategy are based on the present and future needs and expectations of stakeholders.

Areas to address may include:

- *Gathering and understanding information to define the market and market segment the organisation will operate in both now and in the future;*

- *Understanding and anticipating the needs and expectations of customers, employees, partners, society and shareholders, as appropriate;*

- *Understanding and anticipating developments in the market place, including competitor activity.*

 PRIVATE SECTOR Strategic and operational plans are based on information from key stakeholders – staff, partners and suppliers, community and environment, customers and shareholders. Staff information is gathered from annual staff surveys, unit self-assessments, focus groups, coffee meetings with unit heads, team meetings and via a hotline. Information about partners comes from partner reviews, joint workshops and supplier meetings. Community and environment information is collected through staff feedback, local community feedback and group environmental policy. Information concerning customers comes from the annual survey, unit event survey, focus groups and Relationship Managers. Shareholder information is drawn together from group strategy, group strategy reviews, committees, demographic changes, economic factors and audits.

The relevance of the information is checked as part of the planning process and any additional information requirements are identified.

- A comprehensive set of tools, approaches and information sources is used to identify the needs of all key stakeholders.

- This information is understood and taken into account in developing the organisation's policy and strategy.

In a Social Services environment, the need for a systematic approach to using 'service user' and 'carer' surveys was identified at a strategic level, and a number of customised questionnaires were developed to understand and take into account all stakeholders' needs. The results of the surveys are analysed area by area, and service-by-service comparisons are made. They are included in the Bi-monthly Integrated Performance Monitoring report, which is reviewed by senior management as part of a formal review process.

A code of practice for managing the survey work was developed and resulted in an ethical framework being developed. Another policy, based on evidence from survey work, was the provision of a product and service in bulk supplies. This cut transport costs and delivered added service satisfaction. Policy changes are accompanied by user surveys or other forms of consultation to determine their effectiveness.

- A flexible and tailored survey, covering all the services provided by the organisation, identifies customers' needs.

- Examples are given of policies that have been implemented based on understanding and taking into account customer needs and expectations.

 The planning process takes three months and information is gathered from all key stakeholders – customers, staff, local authorities, the community and suppliers. Benchmark information is obtained both nationally and internationally. Changes in sector policy are also taken into account.

Staff keep themselves up to date in their field and are encouraged to conduct annual audits of their project area – the resulting action plans are incorporated in the organisation's development plan. In addition, information from internal audits of people and processes is used in the planning and monitoring process. A draft business plan is issued for consultation with staff and senior managers.

There has been a need for policy changes to reflect government policies and a change in the numbers of people requiring the organisation's services.

- Information is gathered from a range of stakeholders to inform the business planning process.

- Benchmark data and market changes are understood and accounted for in the process.

Criterion 2

3.2 | Policy and Strategy

How the organisation implements its mission and vision via a clear stakeholder-focused strategy, supported by relevant policies, plans, objectives, targets and processes.

Sub-criterion 2B:
Policy and strategy are based on information from performance measures, research, learning and creativity related activities.

Areas to address may include:

- *Collecting and understanding output from internal performance indicators;*

- *Collecting and understanding the output from learning activities;*

- *Analysing the performance of competitors and best in class organisations;*

- *Understanding social, environmental and legal issues;*

- *Identifying and understanding economic and demographic indicators;*

- *Understanding the impact of new technologies;*

- *Analysing and using stakeholders' ideas.*

 PRIVATE SECTOR Strategic and operational plans are based on information from internal measures of current capability and data on external factors in the market place.

Internal information comes from the application of a balanced business scorecard, self-assessments, political, economic, social and technology (PEST), and strengths, weaknesses, opportunities and threats (SWOT) analyses and benchmarking.

Market information is based on the benchmarking of processes and products, group market research, market reports, professional service organisations, widespread internet usage, industry controls, institutes, compliance audits, and UK and global market activity. In addition, participation in regulatory and professional organisations provides further key information.

The information from internal measures and the market is also evaluated as part of the overall planning process.

- Current capability and external factors are all considered in the development of the policy and strategy.

- A comprehensive set of information sources is used, together with several well-recognised tools.

To make informed strategic decisions three analyses are carried out – a needs analysis summarising the needs and expectations of the customers; an environmental analysis of the external factors that drive the organisation; and a competition analysis comparing and contrasting with the competition.

Stakeholder Reports and Monitoring Reports review the changes to the analyses each month, with sources of information for the analyses being extensive. Stakeholder groups keep the organisation aware of the views and levels of satisfaction of the stakeholders. Contract monitoring meetings check how well the organisation is performing to target.

The results are used in a strengths, weaknesses, opportunities and threats (SWOT) analysis, leading to the Mission statement, Critical Success Factors, Strategic Objectives and Strategies. It is resourced and monitored through the business plan.

- The information gathered is comprehensive and reviewed frequently to ensure the policy and strategy reflect any new information, both internally and externally.

 Policy and strategy are based on information collected throughout the year by senior managers, relating to the key process for which they are responsible. Methods used to gather the information include visits to customers and suppliers, customer surveys, team briefings, employee surveys, seminars, visits to other companies, internal performance indicators, benchmarking activities, discussions with the local community, the media and financial advisers, attending exhibitions and reading trade journals.

Information is obtained on Investors in People (IIP), product packaging, bonus structure, reduced waste, new equipment, health and safety legislation and improved delivery. It is discussed at the six-monthly strategic reviews and used to help form policies and strategies relating to employees, productivity, new technologies, increasing market share, controlling costs and current legislation.

- Information collection, to understand current capability and external factors, is an on-going process and includes all key stakeholders.

- New technologies, competitor, social and environmental issues are used to inform the policy and strategy.

Criterion 2

3.2 | Policy and Strategy

How the organisation implements its mission and vision via a clear stakeholder-focused strategy, supported by relevant policies, plans, objectives, targets and processes.

Sub-criterion 2C:
Policy and strategy are developed, reviewed and updated.

Areas to address may include:

- *Developing policy and strategy consistent with the organisation's mission, vision and values and based on the needs and expectations of stakeholders and information from learning and innovation activities;*

- *Balancing the needs and expectations of stakeholders;*

- *Balancing short and long-term pressures and requirements;*

- *Developing alternative scenarios and contingency plans to address risks;*

- *Identifying present and future competitive advantage;*

- *Aligning the organisation's policy and strategy with that of partners;*

- *Reflecting the fundamental concepts of Excellence in policy and strategy;*

- *Evaluating the relevance and effectiveness of policy and strategy;*

- *Identifying critical success factors;*

- *Reviewing and updating policy and strategy.*

 PRIVATE SECTOR To identify how the organisation should compete, the strategic plan is defined from an analysis of the current Vision, Mission and Values, and identification of Critical Success Factors (CSFs).

At the corporate level the Strategy defines intentions for businesses over a two to five-year period. At a basic level these plans define the role which the business will play within the corporate business. The Strategy, in terms of roles, missions and directions, can then be translated into a strategic implementation plan containing targets, events and milestones, and these are used to create an annual plan.

The final strategic plan includes: Mission and Business Environment; Business Objectives and Goals; Trading Contribution; Margins and Value Creation; Strategic Intent; Brand Strategic Roles; Supply Chain; Capital Acquisitions; Customer Development; Innovation Targets; Human Resources and the Organisation; Financial Summary and Risks; Process Milestones and Key Financial Indicators.

- A structured approach and well-recognised tools are used in the development of the policy and strategy.

- The outcome is comprehensive, with milestones and targets, and includes all levels of the organisation.

PUBLIC SECTOR The five-year Strategy, aligned to the Vision, Mission and Values is developed following an annual strategic workshop attended by all senior managers. It includes strengths, weaknesses, opportunities and threats (SWOT) and political, economic, social, technology, legal and environmental (PESTLE) analyses, and a review of input data from stakeholders and the market survey.

An analysis ensures the organisation is capable of delivering the Strategy and, if not, what has to happen to ensure it does. Potential problem analysis is carried out and measures put in place to reduce risk. A business plan is developed, line managers identify resource requirements and senior managers decide priorities. Targets and times are set and progress is monitored at monthly meetings. If any of the processes are not meeting their targets then they are reviewed and, if necessary, changed.

- Following thorough analysis, the organisation clearly defines how it is going to compete.
- There is measurement and review at all stages in the formulation, review and updating process.

 SMALL/MEDIUM The board holds regular Strategic Planning Reviews where the current Strategy is reviewed and decisions for the future are made. Non-executive directors play a critical role in the selection of the strategic choices.

Information is collected through internal analysis and participation in local Business Link initiatives. Both internal performance and external industry information is considered.

The approach has led to the decision to undertake a related diversification to produce another type of product before the market for the current major product becomes more competitive and less profitable. The board is also considering additional options where the company's core competencies may be applied to products in other industries.

Several conclusions and information from the analysis have been shared with customers as part of partnering.

- The strategy has been reviewed and updated, leading to demonstrable business decisions.
- The output is shared with key stakeholders.

Criterion 2

3.2 | Policy and Strategy

How the organisation implements its mission and vision via a clear stakeholder-focused strategy, supported by relevant policies, plans, objectives, targets and processes.

Sub-criterion 2D:
Policy and strategy are deployed through a framework of key processes.

Areas to address may include:

- *Identifying and designing the framework of key processes needed to deliver the organisation's policy and strategy;*

- *Establishing clear ownership of the key processes;*

- *Defining the key processes including the identification of stakeholders;*

- *Reviewing the effectiveness of the framework of key processes to deliver policy and strategy.*

PRIVATE SECTOR

Deployment of the strategy involves converting it into a series of targets using the Strategy Into Action (SIA) goal translation process. The strategic goals are translated in to key performance indicators, and targets are structured on to a business scorecard, based on the Excellence Model, with quadrants for market, organisation, operations and results. These targets are a mixture of outcome measures (e.g. people and customer satisfaction), activity measures (e.g. deliver projects) and process measures (e.g. cost and cycle time reductions). Each strategy (e.g. business, product, country and function) has an associated scorecard.

Part of the SIA process is the development of plans that underpin the scorecard targets. At the team level, there are Team Activity Plans that outline what actions are to be taken to achieve the targets. Individual work plans are agreed from these, and are used as input for setting individual performance targets, which are linked to the achievement of scorecard targets.

- There is a clearly defined, and comprehensive process for deploying the Policy and Strategy throughout the organisation, down to team and individual levels.

- A scorecard tool is used to ensure targets are defined, measured and achieved.

Senior managers were involved in the design and implementation of the Business Management System (BMS), which has the aim of translating and deploying the Policy and Strategy into action through a process framework. Measures are in place to gauge the effectiveness of this goal translation and implementation approach.

The processes lead to a number of outputs, that are compared to the goals to form a closed loop linking back to the stakeholder needs.

Continual review of the measures has led to improvement in the BMS, e.g. an intranet-based electronic BMS has been introduced. As a result of a systematic benchmarking study, the total system is better understood.

- The Policy and Strategy deployment processes are closely linked to stakeholders' needs.

- Following a review of the effectiveness of the deployment process, improvements have been implemented.

 The Aims, Mission and Vision of the business are converted into Policy and Strategy using Deming's Plan-Do-Check-Act cyclical process. This is distilled into a one year Policy and Strategy plan with financial and performance targets.

Deployment of the plan is via a framework of key processes: every manager and team leader has annual objectives as part of their appraisal. These are reviewed early in the year and departmental objectives are cascaded down in line with Policy and Strategy. Departmental managers are also given human resource targets, e.g. training, recruitment and improvement targets.

Success in deployment is reviewed by the management team at quarterly, monthly and weekly meetings. Important inputs to this process are manufacturing and quality performance, raw material costs, sales performance, market intelligence, economic factors and progress on improvement projects.

- Policy and Strategy are deployed as appropriate to the needs of the recipient(s).

- The deployment process is regularly reviewed.

Criterion 2

3.2 | Policy and Strategy

How the organisation implements its mission and vision via a clear stakeholder-focused strategy, supported by relevant policies, plans, objectives, targets and processes.

Sub-criterion 2E:
Policy and strategy are communicated and implemented.

Areas to address may include:

- *Communicating and cascading policy and strategy, as appropriate;*

- *Using policy and strategy as the basis for planning activities and the setting of objectives and targets throughout the organisation;*

- *Aligning, prioritising, agreeing and communicating plans, objectives and targets;*

- *Evaluating the awareness of policy and strategy.*

PRIVATE SECTOR

There is a systematic process for communicating strategy, goals and business plans. After departmental plans have been formulated based on the five-year strategy, a Group Objectives booklet is produced. It contains the goals based on a scorecard approach, the key programmes to deliver the goals and the programme owners, and includes a review of performance against the previous years' goals.

Following its publication, the booklet is cascaded in a systematic way and discussed with every member of staff, focusing on where they fit and the relationship between their objectives and the organisational goals in the Group Objectives booklet. There is space for personal objectives to be slotted in.

A review process confirms deployment of the approach and tests understanding. For the next version the introduction has been expanded to describe the rationale behind the goals and programmes in more detail, which was a direct result of a review into the effectiveness of the approach.

- There is a well-structured and systematic process for communicating and implementing the Policy and Strategy, down to an individual level.

- Improvement actions have been taken to ensure the communication has been properly explained and fully understood.

PUBLIC SECTOR Green and white papers are used to communicate and implement policies. A green paper contains the initial proposal on the need to work up a policy. It is a consultation document, announcing that work is being commissioned. Hard and soft copies (via an intranet) are circulated to all staff, together with presentations to key groups of people. This is followed by the white paper, resulting from the consultation process, and containing the approved new policy, which is also widely circulated.

Implementation involves pilot sites, preparation for change workshops for front-line operational staff and a full pilot evaluation report, including all stakeholders. It contains qualitative and quantitative performance measures, and is evaluated by the senior management team before the policy is approved for full implementation. Each unit then produces an implementation plan to meet the policy changes, which is also approved by senior managers.

- There are systematic and thorough approaches to both the communication and implementation of policies.

- The initial policy proposals, as well as final policies, are communicated for comment.

SMALL/MEDIUM Policy and Strategy are communicated in a number of ways: the Mission statement is on all notice-boards, all new employees are given a copy in their induction pack, all staff attend an annual goal-setting meeting where the linkage to the mission is demonstrated, and this is further reinforced by a company newsletter. Detailed timelines with milestones are raised for all development plans and review meetings are held monthly to check achievements against milestones.

To implement the Policy and Strategy, all staff participate in setting departmental and individual goals, and have a personal goal planner, which they take ownership of and commit to implementing. Their awareness and understanding of the Policy and Strategy is evaluated by several processes including the Excellence Model, an Investors in People (IIP) survey, at their annual appraisal and in the employee survey.

- The Policy and Strategy are communicated and implemented throughout the business.

- It is used as the basis for planning and setting individual's activities.

- The effectiveness of the process is checked in surveys and appraisals.

Criterion 2

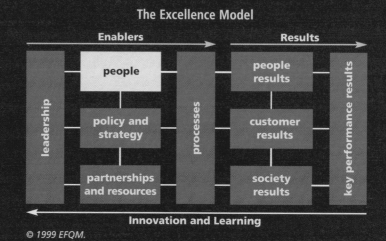

The Excellence Model

Enablers   Results

leadership

people

policy and
strategy

processes

partnerships
and resources

people
results

customer
results

society
results

key performance results

Innovation and Learning

© 1999 EFQM.

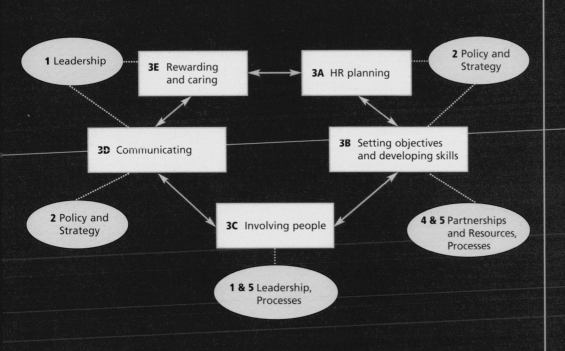

Linkages between
the sub-criteria
and with the
other enablers

3.3 | People

How the organisation manages, develops and releases the knowledge and full potential of its people at an individual, team-based and organisation-wide level, and plans these activities in order to support its policy and strategy and the effective operation of its processes.

Sub-criterion 3A:

People resources are planned, managed and improved.

Areas to address may include:

- *Developing human resource policies, strategies and plans;*

- *Involving employees, and their representatives, in developing human resource policies, strategies and plans;*

- *Aligning the human resource plans with policy and strategy, the organisational structure and the framework of key processes;*

- *Managing recruitment and career development;*

- *Ensuring fairness in all terms of employment, including equal opportunities;*

- *Using people surveys and other forms of employee feedback to improve human resource policies, strategies and plans;*

- *Using innovative organisation methodologies to improve ways of working, e.g. restructuring the supply chain, matrix working, flexible team working, high performance work teams.*

 PRIVATE SECTOR Through a five-year plan, the number of staff are matched with longer-term perspectives linked to business needs. A development and training review group, with representatives from each unit, analyses the skills required by the Quality Plan and Budget. These requirements are prioritised, and all managers evaluate what skills their people have, or will have, and feed proposals back to the review group. Recommendations are given to the Director's Board, who evaluate how any shortfalls will be fulfilled, either in-house or by other methods such as external training or recruitment.

Objectives are cascaded through the approved Quality Plan and Budget, which contains the specific targets and objectives to enable all managers and their teams to create plans to fulfil the resource requirements. A quarterly Development Council monitors the main human resource (HR) programmes, including high potential non-managers and managers development, allowing for a response to changes required by Policy and Strategy reviews.

- The organisation regularly reviews that it has the right number of staff to support its Policy and Strategy and meet the needs of the organisation.

- A structured planning process is used and involves all necessary units.

The human resource (HR) strategy aims to improve delivery of the business objectives through a culture of continuous learning and improvement. It has six key objectives and links to the organisation's culture and values. The human resource plan is aligned to strategy and policy and is monitored for effectiveness and efficiency by a human resource audit plan. Progress against the plans is reported quarterly by the Business Unit Managers. The Executive Team review human resource strategy annually and benchmark best practice companies. Employees are involved with the human resource planning process through Employee Involvement Forums and Staff Surveys. To ensure that the organisation has flexibility, the staff are encouraged to become multi-skilled. Self-directing teams were introduced to allow pooling of resources, and each Business Unit Manager has to identify their resource requirements from the business plan and whether this can be staffed internally or externally.

- There is an HR plan, which is reviewed and audited, to ensure the staff can meet the needs of the business.

- All employees have the opportunity to input into the organisation's HR strategy.

 A three-year strategic view is taken in planning people resources, enabling staff to be matched to customer requirements since 1981 without any redundancies or forced moves. Senior management draw up a human resource (HR) plan, taking into account changing customer needs and numbers. It has sufficient flexibility to allow extra services to be offered as required. Annual variations, analysis of long-term trends, an increase in the complexities of the customers' needs plus feedback from staff development interviews and surveys are used to inform the HR planning process.

Senior management are responsible for the selection, monitoring and development of staff in line with the organisation's policies, and care is taken when recruiting to match skills to the needs, aims and values of the business.

Better use of human resources has been achieved by increasing the emphasis on teamwork.

- A flexible, but structured plan ensure that the organisation's needs are met.

- The needs of key stakeholders – customers – are taken into account.

- Improved ways of working have been introduced.

Criterion 3

3.3 People

H ow the organisation manages, develops and releases the knowledge and full potential of its people at an individual, team-based and organisation-wide level, and plans these activities in order to support its policy and strategy and the effective operation of its processes.

Sub-criterion 3B:
People's knowledge and competencies are identified, developed and sustained.

Areas to address may include:

- *Identifying, classifying and matching people's knowledge and competencies with the organisation's needs;*

- *Developing and using training and development plans to help ensure people match the present and future capability needs of the organisation;*

- *Designing and promoting individual, team and organisational learning opportunities;*

- *Developing people through work experience;*

- *Developing team skills;*

- *Aligning individual and team objectives with the organisation's targets;*

- *Reviewing and updating individual and team objectives;*

- *Appraising and helping people improve their performance.*

 PRIVATE SECTOR Each business unit is responsible for identifying the current and future staff capabilities required to meet business needs. Resource planning is a key step in the approach to business planning. To assist this, all roles within the organisation have a job profile that defines the competencies together with the level of performance required to obtain the next job level. People are encouraged to develop and manage their own development plans, leading to job enrichment and enlargement.

The development needs are identified through discussions with a variety of stakeholders – managers, peers and customers. A systematic process is used to evaluate employees' performance and a key aspect of this process is that it is linked to the organisation's goals, with the output being a development plan.

Many facilities are provided to support the training needs, e.g. formal training and work experience. The organisation also provides self-development workshops.

- People's skills are identified and training is given to ensure the organisation's needs and goals are, and will be, met.

- Both customers and staff are involved in the process.

- A variety of training methods are used to facilitate the process.

The need for the appraisal and development of staff was identified from the results of internal self-assessments against the Excellence Model. This was considered to be a strategic issue that affected all areas of the operation. The human resource function managed the implementation as part of the organisation's Strategic Plan.

Appraisals are conducted annually and all staff are appraised via a formal interview with an employee's immediate boss. The focus is on personal development needs and performance against targets, with personal objectives linked to the organisation's critical success factors (CSFs) and any time relevant needs. A key feature is that the appraisal scheme is not linked to any bonus payments.

Each business unit has a training plan that is reviewed annually on a basis of how much has been delivered.

- The appraisals are linked to the organisation's critical success factors (CSFs).

- The current approach resulted from a review, and the implementation of improvement actions.

 The skill and experience of all staff is classified as Red, Yellow or Green and starts on day one with the induction. To reach Red, staff have to complete their induction in their area. Promotion to Yellow from Red is made when a pre-determined level of competence is achieved, and to Green when two Green-rated people agree that a person is capable of training others.

All staff have an appraisal with a maximum of six months or minimum of one month between them, depending on the individual's requirements. The output is documented by the appraiser on a standard form, and staff prepare by completing a form that includes their main duties linked to Mission and customers, achievement against last year's targets, suggestions for next year's targets, points for discussion and training requirements; a skill chart, tasks lists and training logs are also referred to. Everyone takes part in a voluntary 360° appraisal system.

- The skills and experience of all staff are systematically identified and developed.

- Staff's frequent appraisals are linked to both the organisation's Mission and to the needs of customers.

Criterion 3

3.3 | People

How the organisation manages, develops and releases the knowledge and full potential of its people at an individual, team-based and organisation-wide level, and plans these activities in order to support its policy and strategy and the effective operation of its processes.

Sub-criterion 3C:
People are involved and empowered.

Areas to address may include:

- *Encouraging and supporting individual and team participation in improvement activities;*

- *Encouraging and supporting people's involvement through in-house conferences and ceremonies;*

- *Providing opportunities that stimulate involvement and support innovative and creative behaviour;*

- *Empowering people to take action;*

- *Encouraging people to work together in teams.*

PRIVATE SECTOR

To ensure the organisation is getting the best from its staff, all employees are involved in continuous improvement through best practice schemes. Idea generation, innovation and implementation form part of performance management targets.

Team recognition takes place on a "World Quality Day", where teams are invited to document their achievements. Team members are empowered to nominate their colleagues (including Team Leader and Manager) for exceptional performance. The Managing Director presents the award.

Additionally, an Employee of the Month award is presented. Any individual can vote for any other and the votes go through a panel. One winner per month and two finalists are presented with Edinburgh Crystal, champagne, a certificate and the only reserved car parking space, at the ceremony. An Employee of the Year Award ceremony is held for all monthly winners, their guests and their immediate Manager. The winner receives £1000 worth of holiday vouchers.

- The organisation ensures all employees have the opportunity to get involved in in-house initiatives, and are recognised for it.

- Empowerment and involvement are cultures used to ensure the organisation is getting the best from its people.

- Involvement is linked to employee performance targets.

Staff are involved in project meetings, groups and committees, e.g. information technology (IT) and Quality, and are delegated financial authority to commit money to projects. They are encouraged to participate in improvement activities though the Quality Action Request procedure, which may result in the setting up of a Quality Action Team. The teams comprise staff of mixed work teams and disciplines, have the authority to investigate and make recommendations and have minuted meetings. The effectiveness of these teams is partly monitored by ISO 9001 audits.

There is an annual in-house Quality Event to which around 50% of staff are invited on a rotating basis. Feedback from previous events suggested staff wanted something more interactive, and a workshop of 17 staff was held to come up with a consensus list of Quality Action Requests to put into action.

- Both individual and team participation in improvement activities is encouraged.

- Following a review of the process based on employee feedback, improvement actions were taken.

 People are involved through a key strategic teaming programme. It includes education and training, encouraging staff to be innovative and involved in problem-solving within a self-directed work team environment, goal setting and measurement and team recognition.

The teaming process has evolved to the current situation where empowered teams have very little management involvement and use skills such as Pareto analysis and 8D problem-solving etc.

Empowerment is evidenced by cross-functional, multi-level Quality Improvement Teams, rather than senior managers, overseeing the teaming process, the self-directing work teams planning their own workload in the factory, and a planner as the project leader for a new manufacturing computer control system.

- Involved and empowered teamwork is encouraged at all levels.

- There is evidence of the successful results of this approach.

3.3 | People

How the organisation manages, develops and releases the knowledge and full potential of its people at an individual, team-based and organisation-wide level, and plans these activities in order to support its policy and strategy and the effective operation of its processes.

Sub-criterion 3D:
People and the organisation have a dialogue.

Areas to address may include:

- *Identifying communication needs;*

- *Developing communications policies, strategies and plans based on communications needs;*

- *Developing and using top down, bottom up and horizontal communication channels;*

- *Sharing best practice and knowledge.*

PRIVATE SECTOR

Based on a business area, the 200 top managers attend an annual two-day conference to review and discuss the organisation's past achievements and future targets. The conferences have a central theme, such as innovation and creativity.

In addition, the Business Group President makes special mention of the achievements of teams and individuals within the business group.

A review resulted in the introduction of a video, compact disc and booklet to ensure consistency of the message that is communicated to all staff.

Although one of the main approaches for top-down communication is the formal cascade events that the conference triggers annually, informal events are held on a more regular basis at the operating unit and functional level. These sessions are used for communication and recognition purposes in addition to supporting a culture of involvement through team-based activities focused on current operational issues.

- There are processes for vertical communication at all levels in the organisation.

- Following a review, actions were taken to improve the top-down communication channel.

A number of communication vehicles exist throughout the organisation, some of which have been introduced as a result of areas for improvement identified during self-assessment. These include weekly update newsletters, a national staff newspaper, circulation of key messages from divisional meetings and regular open forums with Business Heads to discuss important issues.

A team undertook reviews of both internal and external communications last year and a number of their recommendations are now being implemented. Principle among these is the creation of a communication strategy and an action plan to deliver.

A trial intranet site was set up, evaluated and is now being developed as a principle source of communicating information.

- Following a review of communications, a wide range of media has been introduced.
- A comprehensive communication strategy is being implemented.

 The Managing Director chairs a weekly meeting of the senior managers to keep them appraised of current issues. These managers then update each other about their area of responsibility. Records are kept of these meetings and actions checked at the next one.

Team briefings take place every two weeks and are the main method of two-way communication between management and employees. They used to be held in the factory, but now occur in a large meeting room. Other members of the senior management team attend these to give up to date information and to listen to feedback from the employees. Team briefing reports are completed and kept on file by the team leader, who reviews comments and decides on appropriate action, e.g. feedback led to a change in the bonus system.

At the end of the financial year, the Managing Director talks to the whole company about past and future growth.

- There are two-way vertical and horizontal communication channels.
- Improvements have been implemented as a result of listening to employees.
- Written records ensure all actions are captured and followed up on.

Criterion 3

3.3 | People

H ow the organisation manages, develops and releases the knowledge and full potential of its people at an individual, team-based and organisation-wide level, and plans these activities in order to support its policy and strategy and the effective operation of its processes.

Sub-criterion 3E:
People are rewarded, recognised and cared for.

Areas to address may include:

- *Aligning remuneration, redeployment, redundancy and other terms of employment with policy and strategy;*

- *Recognising people in order to sustain their involvement and empowerment;*

- *Promoting awareness and involvement in health, safety, the environment and issues on social responsibility;*

- *Setting the levels of benefits, e.g. pension plan, health care, child care;*

- *Promoting social and cultural activities.*

- *Providing facilities and services, e.g. flexible hours, transport.*

 PRIVATE SECTOR To ensure staff are motivated, various recognition schemes are available – some are organisation-wide and others are local initiatives. Examples range from a local award where, for a significant act of customer service, three envelopes are offered, each containing an award, to an annual award that recognises key team players. These teams often include customers and suppliers.

For the annual awards, which are given by the Chief Executive Officer, pictures of the winning teams are taken and displayed in a Hall of Fame. The award process also includes an element of sharing to facilitate learning between teams.

In addition to the non-monetary awards, in some cases stock options are given as a form of reward.

Recognition is also given to long-serving employees, which is marked by a long-service lunch.

- Recognition mechanisms, with different types of reward and aimed at different stakeholder groups, ensure staff motivational levels are such to deliver the organisation's objectives.

- The annual award process contains an element of sharing good practice.

Criterion 3

Annual focus group meetings, involving management and staff representatives, are used to canvass staff's views on reward and recognition outside of the existing pay system. As an outcome of these focus groups, a "good practice guide" for reward and recognition and a system of excellence and long-service awards is being introduced.

Funds of £7.5K are provided to a local nursery to provide economical and competitive child care. This is a popular benefit with staff registering children for a place well in advance of their third birthday (which is the age limit).

When membership to the Fitness Centre dropped, trainers, members and non-members were consulted. Feedback resulted in the introduction of a payment by instalment scheme, and membership increased by 46% the following year.

- Staff's views were considered when reward and recognition was reviewed, and improvements implemented.
- There is evidence of the success of this approach to caring for staff.

 Recognition of the contribution made by staff is always discussed at management meetings and recommendations for recognition are actively sought by the senior managers. In addition, gifts are made available to staff as a special "Thank you" for exceptional achievement, e.g. if they have handled a difficult or challenging situation with initiative and enthusiasm. All customer praise is passed on to individuals with comment forms and letters pinned to the notice-board.

Staff facilities, breaks, meals and accommodation are regularly reviewed with refurbishment of staff amenities often given priority in budgets.

Care, support and counselling are available to those employees with any difficulties from one of the senior managers who is qualified in Counselling and Learning Skills.

- Recognition is given to staff for outstanding performance.
- The needs of the employees are recognised and catered for.
- Recognition from customers is shared and publicised.

Criterion 3

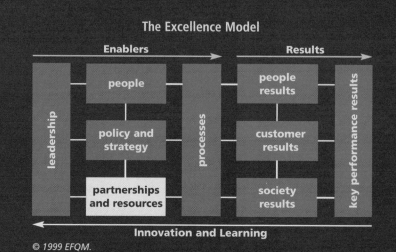

The Excellence Model

Enablers

Results

leadership

people

policy and strategy

partnerships and resources

processes

people results

customer results

society results

key performance results

Innovation and Learning

© 1999 EFQM.

“The organisation's internal resources (e.g. assets) and external resources (e.g. suppliers) are managed to ensure its policy and strategy can be delivered.”

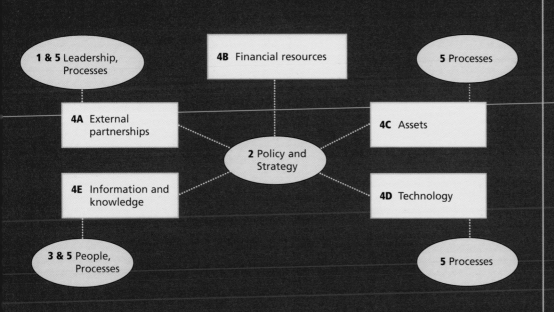

Linkages between the sub-criteria and with the other enablers

3.4 Partnerships and Resources

How the organisation plans and manages its external partnerships and internal resources in order to support its policy and strategy and the effective operation of its processes.

Sub-criterion 4A:
External partnerships are managed.

Areas to address may include:

- *Identifying key partners and strategic partnership opportunities in line with policy and strategy;*

- *Structuring partnership relationships to create and maximise value;*

- *Forming value-adding supply chain partnerships;*

- *Ensuring cultural compatibility and the sharing of knowledge with partner organisations;*

- *Supporting mutual development;*

- *Generating and supporting innovative and creative thinking through the use of partnerships;*

- *Creating synergy in working together to improve processes and add value to the customer/supplier chain.*

 To ensure key partners, support the organisation's goals, a supplier management strategy incorporates the principle of partnership and the commitment to share objectives and resolve problems jointly with suppliers. The process provides a framework for specific improvement processes and activities such as 100% schedule adherence with zero defects. It concentrates on working with suppliers, facilitating improvement in their capability and supports the core purchasing activities.

A Supply Excellence programme has been developed into a company-wide standard. The programme is based on the EFQM Excellence Model® and provides improved vendor quality and delivery performance, opportunities for cost reduction, increased business visibility, sharing of best practice, improved supplier relationships and joint improvement activities.

Supplier evaluation assesses the risk associated with the product, technology and company involved.

- There is a strategy, supported by a sound programme, to develop partnership relationships with key suppliers in support of achieving the organisation's aims and objectives.

- The approach is based on mutual benefit, sharing relevant information and working together.

Criterion 4

All initiatives involving supplier relationships are within European Union (EU) rules and taken to improve the organisation's ability to deliver and achieve value for money for customers. Systems are being developed to match suppliers to individual job requirements to avoid the costly and time-consuming process of open-tendering for every project.

An 'approved' list forms the supplier base, contained within which is a core of more frequently used suppliers. There is a policy to reduce this number, whilst not undermining competition or the ability to satisfy customers. The list was also the subject of an internal benchmarking exercise to create a model of best practice. The business has already implemented most of the 19 points of best practice which came from this exercise.

- Partnership relationships are created with suppliers to form value adding supply chains.

- The aims of the approach are to support the achievement of the company's objectives, plus to increase customer satisfaction.

 To support the policy and strategy, supplier partner relationships are developed. The process includes selecting, prioritising and encouraging continuous improvement with suppliers. They are treated as partners in helping to achieve strategic objectives and to meet/exceed customers' requirements.

Suppliers are included in the project initiation phase to allow their input into the design and development of products. They are also invited into the plant to review processes and charts, attend meetings, encouraged to actively participate in the certification process and are rewarded with recognition and long-term contracts.

The company's supplier council meets bi-monthly and representatives from key suppliers are invited to attend and develop the agenda, giving them direct input into the procurement planning and improvement process.

- An open and sharing partnership exists with key suppliers in support of the policy and strategy.

- Suppliers are involved at several key stages of a project.

- The approach includes the identification of improvements.

Criterion 4

3.4 | Partnerships and Resources

How the organisation plans and manages its external partnerships and internal resources in order to support its policy and strategy and the effective operation of its processes.

Sub-criterion 4B:
Finances are managed.

Areas to address may include:

- *Using financial resources in support of policy and strategy;*

- *Developing and implementing financial strategies and processes;*

- *Evaluating investment in both tangible and non-tangible assets;*

- *Using financial mechanisms and parameters to ensure an efficient and effective resourcing structure;*

- *Managing risks to financial resources.*

PRIVATE SECTOR Financial strategies and plans are part of the business planning process, and the business plan includes the establishment of departmental budgets that support the desired activities. Financial control is devolved to product managers, process owners and budget owners to ensure effective cost management, accountability and optimum use of funds. Both debtors and creditors are managed to achieve cash flow targets, which are key performance indicators. Bad debt is controlled using credit assessment, pre-payments and debt collection programmes, and the credit scoring method that has been developed is based on customers' circumstances rather than historical data.

There is a wide range of performance outcomes, e.g. sales and revenue, and performance indicators, e.g. costs and return on investments. These are monitored against targets. The financial strategies, practices and budgets are regularly reviewed.

- Financial approaches are an integral part of the business planning process, and support both key performance outcomes and indicators.

- Individual processes have been developed to meet internal and external stakeholder needs, e.g. devolution of budget control and credit rating approach.

To support the achievement of the organisation's aims and objectives, finance is monitored by two computer systems. Guidance is available for budget controllers via the financial manual and the procurement quotations and tenders document.

The Divisional Management Team and executive meeting minutes are available to show where monies are spent. The 'Value for Money' directive is followed.

Major projects are costed using a 'ready reckoner' which allows all-inclusive costings, and business cases are used to evaluate expenditure. Risks are managed through contingency fund provision.

Budgets can be flexible and money moved from one area of the budget to another as needs dictate. Funds can also be carried over at the end of the financial year if underspent.

- There is regular and effective monitoring of the financial status in support of the policy and strategy.
- Policy decisions are made by the executive team taking into account the financial strategy, which is appropriate to the needs of the business.

 Financial resources are allocated based on information from the business plan and to meet the key objectives identified in this plan, e.g. investment decisions are taken to support the business plan.

Financial strategies and practices are reviewed annually and improved to ensure they cover all current financial parameters, e.g. an alternative layout for the monthly profit and loss account was introduced to make it easier for non-financial managers to understand and a financial control mechanism has been introduced, allowing the senior managers to know how much profit the business has made on a weekly basis.

A sales rebate system has been agreed with key customers, and all capital expenditure is carefully evaluated for useful life, payback period and funding available. Sensitivity analyses are conducted to determine the risks involved.

- Financial strategies are in place, reviewed and improved to support the achievement of the business plan.
- Risks are managed.
- The approach includes improvements for staff and benefits for customers.

Criterion 4

3.4 Partnerships and Resources

How the organisation plans and manages its external partnerships and internal resources in order to support its policy and strategy and the effective operation of its processes.

Sub-criterion 4C:
Buildings, equipment and materials are managed.

Areas to address may include:

- *Utilising assets in support of policy and strategy;*

- *Managing the maintenance and utilisation of assets to improve total asset life cycle performance;*

- *Managing the security of assets;*

- *Measuring and managing any adverse effects of the organisation's assets on the community and employees (including health and safety);*

- *Optimising material inventories;*

- *Optimising consumption of utilities;*

- *Reducing and recycling waste;*

- *Conserving global non-renewable resources;*

- *Reducing any adverse global impact of products and services.*

 PRIVATE SECTOR

To support the policy and strategy, there is a material management process covering purchasing activities, relationships with its supply base and the physical receipt, on-site storage, quality assurance, handling and preparation of material. The objectives of the material function are to provide material availability to support the agreed levels of customer flexibility and satisfaction, minimise the investment in inventory consistent with the operating objectives, reduce lead-time required to make material available, support the operational and strategic plans, refine and improve the processes which support the materials management activities and continually improve cost competitiveness through cost reduction programmes.

Material is managed and inventories are controlled by a computerised system, which includes material requirements rescheduling, electronic trading, component traceability and bar-coding of suppliers' products. Benchmarking has been undertaken with other locations and suppliers.

- There is a sound approach to ensure material assets support the organisation's objectives, and lead to customer satisfaction.

- Controls and benchmarking are used to monitor and improve the processes.

PUBLIC SECTOR In line with the strategy of a client-focused approach, newly designed work stations are being included within existing buildings. This work is a product of consultation with both staff and customers. The scheme was piloted in two offices before commitment to a full refurbishment programme.

Maintenance on properties is conducted by contractors with guidance from a regional works Consultant. Advisory consultants conduct audits on particular projects and estate surveyors advise on acquisitions and disposal of properties.

Mechanical and electrical contractors conduct monthly visits to offices to carry out planned maintenance programmes.

- Maintenance and utilisation of assets is clearly planned and managed.
- Existing assets are utilised to support developments in policy and strategy.
- Stakeholders – people and customer – are included in the approach.

 SMALL/MEDIUM A number of approaches are used to manage assets in support of the organisation's goals and objectives.

Precise built-in stock control systems are used with monthly stock checks, tight controls on receiving goods, regular rotation of stock and an emphasis on minimum wastage.

Robust stores are used for security, waste is carefully monitored with the use of special bottle banks and environmentally friendly disposal methods, paper is used on both sides, and the minutes of management meetings are distributed on the reverse side of used paper.

Heat, light and power are carefully monitored for optimum facility without waste, and all proposed new equipment is vetted for resource consumption. Power-saving alternatives are used if possible, e.g. an automatically controlled lighting system and water metering.

- Several approaches are evident to optimise the use of material assets and utilities in support of policy.
- The security of assets is also managed.

Criterion 4

3.4 Partnerships and Resources

How the organisation plans and manages its external partnerships and internal resources in order to support its policy and strategy and the effective operation of its processes.

Sub-criterion 4D:
Technology is managed.

Areas to address may include:

- *Identifying and evaluating alternative and emerging technologies in the light of policy and strategy, and their impact on the organisation and society;*

- *Managing the technology portfolio;*

- *Exploiting existing technology;*

- *Innovating technology;*

- *Harnessing technology to support improvement;*

- *Identifying and replacing 'old' technologies.*

PRIVATE SECTOR

The approach to research, development and exploitation of technology is aligned to support the Vision, Policy and Strategy. Technology is managed by the Technology Project Board. At an operational level it is the responsibility of the Director of Advanced Technology and is managed by the Head of Research and Technology and the Research and Technology Operations Manager.

The Technology Plan describes the technologies, how they will be developed and where they are to be applied. The Technology Planning Process collects and evaluates the needs of stakeholders, identifying a balanced set of business benefits, opportunities and the options for their achievement. This allows measured judgements to be made on how available funding can be maximised. The process for the creation of the plan and the plan for the following year are reviewed and developed annually. The plan must link Research and Technology activity to business need, and be matched to the project timescales for technology insertion.

- There is a clear strategy for managing and exploiting technology in support of the organisation's objectives.

- The approach takes customers' needs into account, and is supported by processes.

Intellectual property of in-house systems is being exploited.

PUBLIC SECTOR

Business intelligence is supplied to customers under a contract which ensures that the copyright, and all other intellectual property rights, remain with the organisation.

A manager has been appointed to act as a focal point to co-ordinate the requirements of the staff within the organisation and its customers.

Desktop publishing has been introduced to save time and money (approx. £10,000 p.a.) to increase the organisation's capability for producing customer newsletters. These inform the partners of progress on major items.

- The organisation is exploiting its existing technology systems on a commercial basis.
- The approaches are taking customers' needs into account.

 Through workshops and in-house continuous improvement discussion groups it was agreed that the business needed to use technology more fully. A programme of network linkup was successfully implemented, linking all the users, whilst maintaining the existing platforms that their software was designed to run on.

SMALL/MEDIUM

There is now a company website, an e-mail system, with public access folders, resulting in less paper in circulation, and an e-mail spares ordering service for the 'high tech' section of the customer base.

The next aim is a web page for customer information, to be a technical reference site and full spare parts ordering service. The target is to have a company icon on every customer's personal computer for linkup to information, stock, new products and services.

- In support of the business goals, technology improvements have been implemented, and more are planned.
- Following reviews with key stakeholders, alternative technologies were evaluated, and old technologies replaced.

Criterion 4

85

3.4 | Partnerships and Resources

How the organisation plans and manages its external partnerships and internal resources in order to support its policy and strategy and the effective operation of its processes.

Sub-criterion 4E:
Information and knowledge are managed.

Areas to address may include:

- *Collecting, structuring and managing information and knowledge in support of policy and strategy;*

- *Providing appropriate access, for both internal and external users, to relevant information and knowledge;*

- *Assuring and improving information validity, integrity and security;*

- *Cultivating, developing and protecting unique intellectual property to maximise customer value;*

- *Seeking to acquire, increase and use knowledge effectively;*

- *Generating innovative and creative thinking within the organisation through the use of relevant information and knowledge resources.*

 PRIVATE SECTOR To support policy and strategy, information and knowledge are managed by an account management approach. This approach sits within an agreed account plan covering business strategy, process improvements and resource requirements.

Information is available through the intranet and through a common network mounted file server. Two main intranet homepages cover design and the manufacturing area, and an employee homepage is also available through terminals in the restaurant, tea-bars and PCs. It provides common access to online reports, training material and performance figures against the key measures for the site.

Data accuracy is reviewed, and error reports from automated scripts ensure database referential integrity; the results are e-mailed automatically to the system administrator for analysis and correction. Network monitoring assures the proactive design of the network, suitability of the bandwidth and latency between sites, and security. Disaster recovery plans are in place and are tested regularly.

- Knowledge and information are clearly well managed so that key stakeholders have ready and easy access to it.

- The approach is closely linked to supporting the achievement of the organisation's strategy.

A dedicated information department was created to provide easy corporate access to complex information, such as strategic information on the way the organisation is operating.

Use is made of information systems both within and outside the immediate control of the organisation, promoting and funding the use of external data collection. The aim is to make this data as widely available as possible on the most appropriate basis to improve general understanding and increase efficiency. This is validated by questions in the employee survey.

Each internal application is accompanied by prescribed internal controls to ensure that data is completely and accurately entered, master file integrity is maintained, and that processing and reporting can be validated.

- There is clear evidence of a sound approach to strategic information management.

- Data from relevant information systems is widely circulated.

- There are controls to ensure accuracy and integrity of data.

 Information is structured and managed to support policies such as the service provided to customers, and to facilitate management of internal processes, e.g. customer support and staff development.

Information on each customer is vital to identify specific needs and is used to aid communication, planning and monitor progress. A personal record for each customer is kept.

Information to maintain service quality includes weekly planning sheets, used to monitor what is being delivered and how it is adapted to meet the needs of the specific customers; also to ensure continuity of service delivery if a member of staff is not available.

Information on staff is kept on computer databases, and other sources of information include the results of customer surveys that are available to all staff.

- Information is collected and managed to inform policy and strategy.

- The approach is used for the benefit of key stakeholders – customers and staff.

Criterion 4

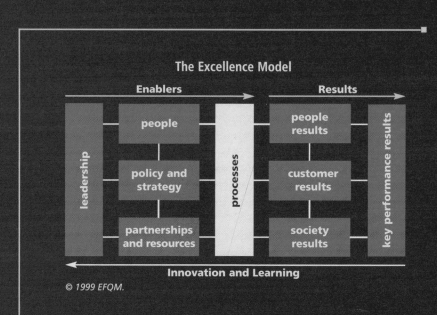

The Excellence Model

Enablers

Results

leadership

people

policy and
strategy

partnerships
and resources

processes

people
results

customer
results

society
results

key performance results

Innovation and Learning

© 1999 EFQM.

"The organisation has key processes, which are reviewed and improved, to ensure the policy and strategy can be delivered for the benefit of all stakeholders."

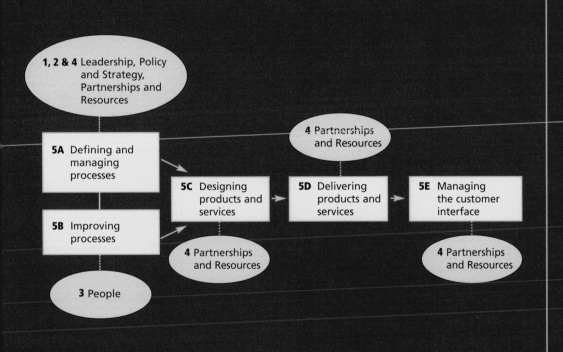

1, 2 & 4 Leadership, Policy and Strategy, Partnerships and Resources

5A Defining and managing processes

5B Improving processes

3 People

4 Partnerships and Resources

5C Designing products and services

4 Partnerships and Resources

5D Delivering products and services

5E Managing the customer interface

4 Partnerships and Resources

Linkages between the sub-criteria and with the other enablers

3.5 | Processes

How the organisation designs, manages and improves its processes in order to support its policy and strategy and fully satisfy, and generate increasing value for, its customers and other stakeholders.

Sub-criterion 5A:
Processes are systematically designed and managed.

Areas to address may include:

- *Designing the organisation's processes, including those key processes needed to deliver policy and strategy;*

- *Establishing the process management system to be used;*

- *Applying systems standards covering, e.g. quality systems such as ISO 9000, environmental systems, occupational health and safety systems in process management;*

- *Implementing process measures and setting performance targets;*

- *Resolving interface issues inside the organisation and with external partners for the effective management of end-to-end processes.*

 PRIVATE SECTOR Processes are systematically designed and managed. The key processes and support processes that enable achievement of the vision are identified, together with appropriate measures.

Each key process is assigned an owner, responsible for developing and improving the process and for implementing necessary changes to system applications. Weekly meetings, chaired by the Business Process Director, are used to review change programme progress, discuss process improvement opportunities and analyse the impact of IT developments on the key processes. They are also responsible for ensuring that process changes are written into procedures and incorporated into the Quality Management System.

More radical changes to the business are managed as projects, and business cases are submitted to the senior management team for approval. Cross-functional teams deal with interfaces between processes and process mapping is used to understand and document key process steps.

- The organisation bases its management approach on the effective management of key processes.

- Each key process has an owner with the responsibility and authority to develop and improve the process.

- It is incorporated into the Quality Management System.

PUBLIC SECTOR

A top-level process map was developed, comprising four components:

- Provide direction and improvement

- Satisfy customer needs

- Manage the capability of the organisation

- Measure and improve performance.

Each of these top-level processes has a defined set of sub-processes. Process owners have been identified at board level with local process owners at operational level.

Process management is an integral part of the Business Management System (BMS), which covers areas such as ISO 9000, ISO 14000, Investors in People (IIP), Finance Controls and Health, Safety and Environment (HSE) policies. A balanced set of qualitative and quantitative measures is used to measure process performance and effectiveness at delivering policy and strategy. They are linked to other measurement approaches, e.g. the people survey.

- There are well-defined and developed processes with a clear rationale.

- Key processes are an integral part of the BMS, which is deployed across the organisation.

- Measurement occurs to monitor process performance and identify necessary improvement actions.

SMALL/MEDIUM

Flowcharts are used to manage all processes, and overview flowcharts have been developed for all the functional areas. These simple flowcharts show the natural flow of product or information through the departments, and each activity step is decomposed to a lower level of detail.

The flowcharts are displayed at the point of use, and are also available on the main computer system. They form part of the Quality Management System (QMS), coming under the system's change control disciplines.

Each product has a 'Device History Record', which shows the production steps and records the relevant Quality Control checks for the batch. The 'Device History Record' also references the relevant flowcharts that should be followed during product manufacture.

- Processes are fully documented as an integral part of the Quality Management System.

- Flowcharts are used to communicate processes and encourage process thinking across departmental boundaries.

- All activities are covered, including administrative activities.

Criterion 5

3.5 | Processes

How the organisation designs, manages and improves its processes in order to support its policy and strategy and fully satisfy, and generate increasing value for, its customers and other stakeholders.

Sub-criterion 5B:
Processes are improved, as needed, using innovation in order to fully satisfy and generate increasing value for customers and other stakeholders.

Areas to address may include:

- *Identifying and prioritising opportunities for improvement, and other changes, both incremental and breakthrough;*

- *Using performance and perception results and information from learning activities to set priorities and targets for improvement and improved methods of operation;*

- *Stimulating and bringing to bear the creative and innovative talents of employees, customers and partners in incremental and break through improvements;*

- *Discovering and using new process designs, operating philosophies and enabling technology;*

- *Establishing appropriate methods for implementing change;*

- *Piloting and controlling the implementation of new or changed processes;*

- *Communicating process changes to all appropriate stakeholders;*

- *Ensuring people are trained to operate new or changed processes prior to implementation;*

- *Ensuring process changes achieve predicted results.*

 PRIVATE SECTOR When a process is undergoing a review, a process improvement team is established. This includes a cross-section of people who operate and manage the process, and utilise its output. The team is managed by a process developer who works closely with the process owner. Key processes are owned at board level. The team members are trained in the techniques of process improvement. General guidelines regarding the management of improvement teams are included within the Quality Management System documentation.

The process used for problem-solving is a cycle consisting of the following steps: identify problem, gather data, analyse data, generate solutions, select the solution, plan for implementation, implement, review and continue.

Creativity and innovation are core competencies within the Annual Performance Review and in personal development plans. Customer and supplier feedback provides regular input for the improvement processes.

- There is a simple and effective process for improving the organisation's processes.

- Process improvement teams represent all process stakeholders.

- The process improvement culture is reinforced by links to personal development and targets.

The need for improvements to a key care management process was identified at a strategic level and this need was reinforced by the results of internal self-assessments against the Excellence Model. The process covers how customer needs are assessed, agreeing a plan, implementing, monitoring and reviewing it. It was re-engineered to create a differentiated approach – customers with simple needs could use a simple process, e.g. a help-desk, whilst those with complex needs would receive intensive service via a more complex process.

The proposed changes were widely circulated in a paper, then a full implementation plan issued for consultation, addressing the needs of all stakeholders, and including clear benefits and reasons for the change. A pilot implementation is now underway, involving reorganising management, office bases and teams, and there is a human resource plan for people skills and competencies.

- The approach reinforces the principles of 'Best Value', and includes customer focus, consultation and comparisons.

- It addresses a current need and has a direct link with the Policy and Strategy.

- There is a clear process and the change was implemented in a structured way.

 A workshop was held on waste management to identify time wasted, unnecessary movement and handling, duplication of effort, damaged goods, etc. As a result of this workshop, a production team planned, proposed and executed a complete factory reorganisation to improve the flow of capital equipment orders from goods inwards through fabrication to despatch.

They also undertook a clean-up, clear-up and get organised exercise on the factory floor, reviewing adequacy of tools and their storage. They introduced trolleys at work bays to eliminate the time and disruption caused by fitters walking to and from the stores when they ran out of low cost basic items. This reduced non-productive time for the fitters, and the needless repetitive booking out of low value items by the stores staff. It also enabled them to concentrate time on rolling inventory of the more expensive components.

- Both incremental and breakthrough opportunities for improvement were identified and implemented.

- Employees affected by the changes were fully involved in the process improvement exercise.

Criterion 5

3.5 | Processes

How the organisation designs, manages and improves its processes in order to support its policy and strategy and fully satisfy, and generate increasing value for, its customers and other stakeholders.

Sub-criterion 5C:
Products and services are designed and developed based on customer needs and expectations.

Areas to address may include:

- *Using market research, customer surveys and other forms of feedback to determine customer needs and expectations for products and services both now and in the future, and their perceptions of existing products and services;*

- *Anticipating and identifying improvements aimed at enhancing products and services in line with customers' future needs and expectations;*

- *Designing and developing new products and services to address the needs and expectations of customers;*

- *Using creativity and innovation to develop competitive products and services;*

- *Generating new products with partners.*

The company uses a product innovation process with a funnel approach comprising five phases:

- Ideas – ideas are generated
- Feasibility – ideas are transformed into reality
- Capability – ability to produce the product is determined
- Launch – the product is available
- Post-launch evaluation – the product is on the market.

Ideas are generated from many sources, including board review, technology development or an idea from a customer or employee. All are evaluated by extensive primary market research involving business representatives with direct customer contact.

The process is used for all product development from product enhancements through to 'breakthroughs', dependent on the extent of the innovation. A clear customer benefit has to be identified that will lead to a definite business benefit before ideas are authorised to pass from the ideas phase to the feasibility phase.

Following a review of the process, improvements include a clarification of roles and responsibilities at each decision point.

- The process is used throughout the business to develop products for both global and local markets.

- Ideas for new products come from several sources and are thoroughly reviewed, based on customer needs and expectations.

- Annual plan targets and scorecard targets have been met in company innovation reviews.

A specific role in promoting innovative solutions has been adopted to tackle some of the historically ingrained business problems.

Grants are provided to sponsor innovative research proposals which address relevant issues. Examples of these include testing of energy efficient and ecologically sound concepts, and "smart" products to foster independence for disabled people.

The business is also innovating projects which deal with the economy and communities. This can include developing ideas generated internally or piloting foreign initiatives in a regional context.

Examples of this include a collaborative project with the Danish Government, and providing social and training facilities that were originally developed in France.

- There are clear examples of a structured and innovative approach to solving issues identified through feedback.

- The organisation is designing and developing new products to address their customers' current and future needs.

 The primary focus for product improvement is customer satisfaction. Customer comments, complaints and suggestions are used to identify potential improvements to services and facilities. They are systematically recorded, and customers are kept informed of what action is being taken. New ideas and significant improvements to a process can be tested during the low season, so they are tried and trusted during the high season.

Product and service performance are frequently reviewed against national trends, and both local and national competition. All employees are invited to experience the company's products and services out of season to assess the quality and service they themselves provide. They are also given the opportunity to do the same at other quality establishments.

- Employees and customers are involved in the design and development of products and services.

- Benchmarking is used to compare competitive performance.

- Process, service and product changes are piloted in a low-risk environment.

Criterion 5

3.5 | Processes

How the organisation designs, manages and improves its processes in order to support its policy and strategy and fully satisfy, and generate increasing value for, its customers and other stakeholders.

Sub-criterion 5D:
Products and services are produced, delivered and serviced.

Areas to address may include:

- *Producing or acquiring products and services in line with designs and developments;*

- *Communicating, marketing and selling products and services to existing and potential customers;*

- *Delivering products and services to customers;*

- *Servicing products and services, where appropriate.*

PRIVATE SECTOR

Strong brand image is used to give credibility to new products and entry into new markets. Substantial resource is allocated to building and maintaining the brand, e.g. billboard posters, award winning TV advertising, and sponsorship of local community activities. Brand strength is monitored through feedback from customers and society.

The organisation/customer interface is regularly reviewed and improved, e.g. restructuring the sales areas to focus on key accounts and an initiative to improve consistency of contact by organisation of the work allocation.

Measures are in place to monitor the delivery of the service, e.g. the call centre call quality, customer support and field sales services quality, plus the delivery of the tangible aspects of the product. A call centre has been established, with leading edge telecommunication methods, to verify and enhance the core data and thereby ensure integrity of the products.

- All aspects of service delivery are covered by the approach, including the customer interface, quality of delivered product and integrity of information.

- The approaches are supported by a range of results measures.

- New product credibility is established through links with a strong brand image.

With 20 offices covering five regions, the devolved organisation means that the business works closely with local authority and private sector bodies, as well as the local community, to develop effective solutions for home ownership on the ground.

To ensure all offices work to clear and consistent standards of delivery, there is a Process Improvement Network Group to bring together managers from across the organisation to identify priority areas for improvement and to encourage the adoption of best practice; in addition, regular strategies for IT, staffing and training are derived, and periodic audits of the business' internal control system are conducted.

- The organisation is structured for the effective delivery and servicing of customers' requirements.

- The approach is deployed throughout the organisation, with controls in place to ensure consistent implementation.

 The business has identified design and innovation skills as an area of advantage over the competition. The new product design process was re-engineered, using a cross-functional team, to maximise performance in four areas:

- Provide customers with a quick and accurate quotation

- Ensure the customer's product brief was clearly understood and communicated

- Undertake rigorous risk assessment and verification at all stages of the design process

- Quickly achieve quality capable of full production status.

The process is monitored for a number of parameters, e.g. lead-time to quote, and improvements made.

A project manager is responsible for ensuring all new projects are well managed, have a clear brief and involve the appropriate team.

- There is a clear process to ensure products are developed in line with customers' requirements.

- The processes are reviewed and improvements made.

- There are links to key performance results and stakeholder satisfaction.

Criterion 5

3.5 Processes

How the organisation designs, manages and improves its processes in order to support its policy and strategy and fully satisfy, and generate increasing value for, its customers and other stakeholders.

Sub-criterion 5E:
Customer relationships are managed and enhanced.

Areas to address may include:

- *Determining and meeting customers' day-to-day contact requirements;*

- *Handling feedback received from day-to-day contacts including complaints;*

- *Proactive involvement with customers to discuss and address their needs, expectations and concerns;*

- *Following up on sales, servicing and other contacts to determine levels of satisfaction with products, services and other customer sales and servicing processes;*

- *Seeking to maintain creativity and innovation in the customer sales and servicing relationship;*

- *Using regular surveys, other forms of structured data gathering and data gathered during day-to-day customer contacts in order to determine and enhance customer relationship satisfaction levels.*

 PRIVATE SECTOR

A Customer Relations Unit develops proactive processes to support customer retention. Besides contacting customers to meet their specific needs, a quarterly telephone survey is undertaken which provides the Customer Relations Unit with information to identify areas for new or improved processes.

Customer Focus Groups are formed to check customer priorities as researched through the customer surveys; to identify any possible cross-functional issues; to understand specific customer issues and to test new product development ideas. More specific marketing initiatives have also used customer focus groups to gain both customer preference and immediate feedback.

Complaints are recorded at unit level by unit complaints co-ordinators. A systematic approach is used to identify each unit's most common issue. Brainstorming is used to identify solutions and improve procedures.

- The company displays a high level of commitment to managing customer relationships.

- Customers are involved extensively in monitoring and improving performance, and in product development.

- Measures are applied throughout.

Regular surveys of customer satisfaction have been commissioned over a number of years, and the approach has evolved over time to reflect the key changes to the business. In addition, clients are invited to participate in group discussions and one-to-one interviews.

The introduction of a new strategy has involved extensive client consultation and the perceptions and needs of the client group have informed its design and planning. Improvements were made to the implementation as a result of this process.

Data on complaints, suggestions and compliments are collated at district, regional and national level. The data are checked for trends which may indicate a problem with policy or procedure. Improvements in guidance or procedure are then considered at national level.

- A structured approach exists to the collection and analysis of day-to-day feedback resulting in national improvements.

- There is proactive involvement with clients to discuss and address their needs.

- A structured approach exists to improve client relationships.

 To help meet stakeholders' contact requirements, a monthly newsletter is circulated to current and past customers, staff, suppliers, local authorities and institutions to inform, educate, influence and celebrate.

Customer surveys were started to identify the organisation's strengths and scope for improvement. An open-door policy operates for customers who are encouraged to telephone or visit if they have concerns. Where possible an appointment will be made for the same day and taken by the departmental manager.

Visits are made to a new customer's premises before starting business to assess their needs in advance. Monthly meetings are held with local authorities and boards to ensure the business is meeting their requirements.

- There is tangible evidence that the business cares and listens to the views of its customers.

- Customers are encouraged to communicate with the business.

- This has clear links to the values of the organisation in Policy and Strategy.

Criterion 5

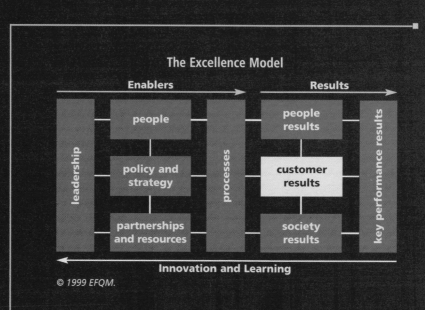

The Excellence Model

Enablers

Results

leadership

people

policy and
strategy

partnerships
and resources

processes

people
results

customer
results

society
results

key performance results

Innovation and Learning

© 1999 EFQM.

“The organisation's achievements with respect to its customers, based on their opinions and the organisation's measures.”

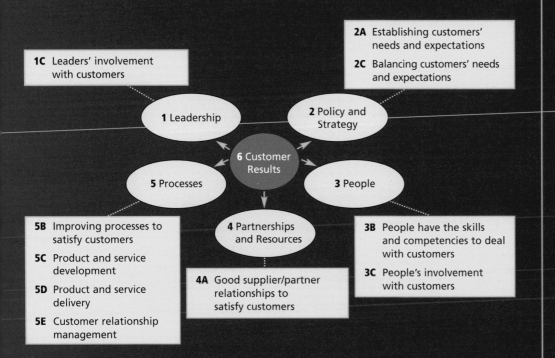

2A Establishing customers' needs and expectations

2C Balancing customers' needs and expectations

1C Leaders' involvement with customers

1 Leadership

2 Policy and Strategy

6 Customer Results

5 Processes

3 People

5B Improving processes to satisfy customers

5C Product and service development

5D Product and service delivery

5E Customer relationship management

4 Partnerships and Resources

4A Good supplier/partner relationships to satisfy customers

3B People have the skills and competencies to deal with customers

3C People's involvement with customers

Linkages with the enablers

3.6 | Customer Results

What the organisation is achieving in relation to its external customers.

Sub-criterion 6A:
Perception measures.

Areas to address may include:

- *Overall image – accessibility, communication, flexibility, proactive behaviour, responsiveness;*

- *Products and services – quality, value, reliability, design innovation, delivery, environmental profile;*

- *Sales and after-sales support – capabilities and behaviour of employees, advice and support, customer literature and technical documentation, handling complaints, product training, response time, technical support, warranty and guarantee provisions;*

- *Loyalty – intention to repurchase, willingness to purchase other products and services from the organisation, willingness to recommend the organisation.*

 PRIVATE SECTOR To establish the views, needs and priorities of customers, a range of tools and approaches is used to capture direct feedback, including focus groups, surveys and complaints. This feeds through into the development of Policy and Strategy and the improvement of processes. All indicators are compared against benchmarks and targets.

The satisfaction score the previous year showed that the organisation was performing at the best in class level and the following year it performed higher. Besides overall customer satisfaction with the organisation and unit, the following indicators are used: reputation of company; efficient response to enquiries; helpfulness of customer contact staff; knowledgeable telephone staff; ability of staff to provide information quickly and to keep you informed of any changes; paperwork written in plain English, and easy to complete paperwork.

All targets have shown a year-on-year improvement and in many areas are best in class.

- There is a comprehensive set of feedback measures to determine the customers' judgement of the organisation.

- The results are mapped against targets and benchmarks, and are used to identify improvement activities and inform the Policy and Strategy.

Criterion 6

PUBLIC SECTOR Direct customer feedback in a recent report ranked the organisation within the top three regionally and in the top ten nationally by its customers. It was graded 1 (outstanding) in its responsiveness to customers. Nationally only 14 out of 456 organisations were graded 1 for their Quality Assurance programmes.

In customer satisfaction, the organisation has achieved all of its set targets over five years. The strategic Business Unit received 100% satisfactory grading by its customers in all but two areas and these areas scored 99.99%. Only nine customer complaints have been received in a four year period.

The organisation has identified all its customers and set measurement targets. Customer surveys are carried out annually to assess customer satisfaction and to identify areas for improvement.

- There is a systematic approach to measuring the customers' perception of the organisation.

- Results show there has been a positive trend over five years and are favourable when compared with competitors.

SMALL/MEDIUM Customer satisfaction is key to two of the company's objectives – continuous profitable growth and business improvement.

Feedback in customer surveys indicates overall satisfaction levels rose 10% over two years and are 10% above target. Highest results are obtained in the overall image category, scoring 85%, also one of the most improved categories, rising from 68%. As a result of an improvement, with customers speaking directly to the production scheduler, the rating of the business for effective communication also rose from 62% to 83%; rises recorded include flexibility (75% to 88%), responding to needs (70% to 85%), overall products and services (75% to 78%), product quality (75% to 79%), delivery on time (68% to 76%), sales/after sales support (68% to 78%), professionalism of staff (69% to 89%), technical support (67% to 78%) and overall loyalty (69% to 83%).

- Customer perception measures are comprehensive, show a positive trend and can be linked to improvement activities that have occurred.

Criterion 6

3.6 | Customer Results

W hat the organisation is achieving in relation to its external customers.

Sub-criterion 6B:
Performance indicators.

Areas to address may include:

- *Overall image – number of customer accolades and nominations for awards, press coverage;*

- *Products and services – competitiveness, defect, error and rejection rates, guarantee provisions and warranty provisions, complaints, logistic indicators, product life cycle, innovation in design, time to market;*

- *Sales and after-sales support – demand for training, handling of complaints, response rates;*

- *Loyalty – duration of relationship, effective recommendations, frequency/value of orders, lifetime value, number of complaints and compliments, new and/or lost business, customer retention.*

 The organisation reports internal measures on PRIVATE SECTOR customer satisfaction by comparing all indicators against benchmarks and targets, which are driven by industry standards.

The predictors used are:

- Customer retention rates by product

- Market indicators

- Customer conversion rates by unit

- Quality of correspondence

- Professionalism of staff

- Complaint handling

- Press coverage in terms of positive articles.

An independent company is employed to sample external correspondence and feedback on the clarity of letters against a plain English standard. Each unit receives their results to enable them to address issues specific to them. The analysis shows good improvements over a period of five years, e.g. the results in the "strong/good" category of the letters increased from below 60% to more than 90% four years later.

- There is a comprehensive set of performance indicators by which the company can make internal judgements about its customers' satisfaction levels.

- There is evidence that improvements are made.

Performance indicators have shown that information technology product and service price reductions are a key priority each year. As a result, a number of projects have been undertaken to improve efficiency without adversely affecting quality. The efficiencies resulting from these projects have been passed on to the customer in the form of price reductions. The Price Index, where the distribution of price reductions across the range of products and services being agreed with the customer, has reduced year on year over a four-year period.

The key performance target – % delivery of services to customers to service levels for budget, time, and quality as agreed within contracts has improved year on year from 94.5% (target = 80%) to 99% (target = 92%) two years later.

- The organisation has used the results from its performance indicator measures to effect improvements and share the financial benefits with customers.

- There is evidence of positive trends over a four-year period and that targets have been met or exceeded.

 An internal judgement of customer satisfaction is the very high level of repeat business due to personal recommendations that the business sustains – from around 900 bookings, nearly 500 were repeat business and over 200 were as a result of a personal recommendation. As reported in the industry monthly surveys, the business has consistently performed well above average in key measures for three years, across all areas of customer satisfaction, when compared with regional standards, including larger businesses.

Of the 800 customer comment forms completed 99% were complimentary with 9% also adding suggestions for improvement, and only 1% registered a complaint; 15,590 products were sold and only 55 (0.4%) gave rise to any negative comment.

- A key predictor of customer satisfaction is their loyalty, and improvements are based on customer comments.

- There are very low levels of complaint.

Criterion 6

The Excellence Model

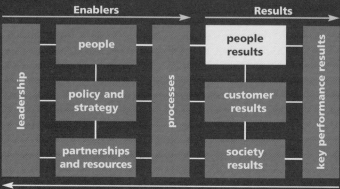

"The organisation's achievements with respect to its employees, based on their opinions and the organisation's measures."

2A Establishing people's needs and expectations

2C Balancing people's needs and expectations

2E Communicating policy and strategy

1D Leaders' involvement with people

1 Leadership

2 Policy and Strategy

7 People Results

5 Processes

3 People

5B Supporting people with process change

4 Partnerships and Resources

4E Ensuring people have access to the information and knowledge needed to do their job

3A Planning and managing people

3B Identifying, developing and sustaining people skills

3D Organisational communications with people

3E Rewarding, recognising and caring

Linkages with the enablers

3.7 | People Results

What the organisation is achieving in relation to its people.

Sub-criterion 7A:
Perception measures.

Areas to address may include:

- *Motivation – career development, communication, empowerment, equal opportunities, involvement, leadership, opportunity to learn and achieve, recognition, target setting and appraisal, the organisation's values, vision, mission, policy and strategy, training and development;*

- *Satisfaction – organisation's administration, employment conditions, facilities and services, health and safety conditions, job security, pay and benefits, peer relationships, the management of change, the organisation's environmental policy and impact, the organisation's role in the community and society, working environment.*

PRIVATE SECTOR

To gauge employee perceptions, a national survey, with a wide range of measures, is conducted by the parent organisation, thus allowing comparisons with internal data. Targets have been set for overall results, plus by groups of questions, e.g. reward and recognition, working environment and managers. Three indices are also derived from the survey results – for managers' performance, people satisfaction and quality of life. This latter measure has a clear link to the approaches for employee care. All measures are linked to scorecards and current performance shows an improving trend over a four-year period with targets met and good comparison with benchmarks.

A review showed that monitoring needed to be more frequent to support planning activities. A local quarterly survey was introduced, with 19 questions and to a 20% staff sample at random and it received a response rate of around 60%. A further refinement is that it is aligned to the main corporate-wide survey.

- An extensive range of measures is collected to determine employees' judgement of all aspects of the operation.

- There is evidence of the use of a scorecard tool for assessing the results.

Since 1988, an annual staff survey has been conducted nationally and administered externally. The survey is directed by a steering group of people from both local and regional offices as well as from head office.

The business receives the results for the organisation as a whole, thus allowing it to benchmark regional results against other regions. All nine regions are allocated targets using the same model and the business' results benchmark well against the national average, with a lead of 5%, which is considered to be of high statistical significance.

- Targets for people judgement are set and achieved.

- The business compares favourably with national averages for employee perception results.

 Employee perceptions are gathered from bi-annual surveys and six-monthly personal development plan meetings.

The overall satisfaction rating in a survey was 77%, up from 69% two years previously. The main reason for this improved result is that, following the earlier survey, a Human Resource Director was appointed to work towards Investors in People (IIP).

Satisfaction levels are sought on areas including training and development needs (76%, up from 69% over two years), keeping staff informed (90%, up from 74%), encouraged to develop ideas (79%, up from 71%), recognition for performance (80%, up from 69%), and physical working conditions (90%, up from 70%).

In the later survey, employees were asked if they thought management would act on problems identified in the survey, and over 80% responded positively.

- Employee perception data is collected regularly, both formally and informally.

- There is evidence and example that the feedback is acted upon.

- The results indicate that actions relating to people, e.g. training, recognition, are being taken.

Criterion 7

3.7 People Results

What the organisation is achieving in relation to its people.

Sub-criterion 7B:
Performance indicators.

Areas to address may include:

- *Achievements – competency requirements versus competencies available, productivity, success rates of training and development to meet objectives;*

- *Motivation and involvement – involvement in improvement teams, involvement in suggestion schemes, levels of training and development, measurable benefits of teamwork, recognition of individuals and teams, response rates to people surveys;*

- *Satisfaction – absenteeism and sickness levels, accident levels, grievances, recruitment trends, staff turnover, strikes, use of benefits, use of organisation provided facilities, (e.g. recreational, crèche);*

- *Services provided to the organisation's people – accuracy of personnel administration, communication effectiveness, speed of response to enquiries, training evaluation.*

 PRIVATE SECTOR Company-wide performance measures relating to people are distributed to each business unit, together with specific feedback on their own area compared to the company norm. The categories measured include employee involvement, leadership, management practices, training and development, performance management, workload and stress, customer focus, continuous improvement, compensation, company image and pride, competitive position, working relationships, communication and job security. Additionally each unit receives a copy of the comments made by staff in their area. Both the overall company results and the specific unit results are communicated to staff. Managers and staff then work together to decide on actions to address their main areas for improvement.

A scheme monitors employee improvement ideas and compares the number of ideas raised with the number of ideas implemented. Staff receive a full explanation if an idea cannot be implemented.

- The organisation judges its people satisfaction using a wide variety of categories relevant to key stakeholders.

- The results compared with industry norms and benchmarks, are communicated to all staff.

Criterion 7

One of the most important performance indicators measured by the organisation is the investment made in the training and developing the people – 4.9% of the total salary bill, compared with an average spend of 2.6% in service industry companies. It equates to £652 per employee, compared to an average of £319 in the service industry.

Although the value of investment in training has remained constant over a five-year period, more courses are being run and more people are involved, but costs are lower. This is due to the customisation of external material and the delivery of more in-house courses.

Key indicators of people satisfaction include absenteeism, staff turnover and recruitment. These measures show positive trends over a three-year period with favourable comparisons to other similar units.

- A key performance indicator for judging people satisfaction has been identified, measured and actions taken to improve the service available for the benefit of the organisation and its people.

- Comparisons with the industry average are favourable.

 Several measures have been selected as key indicators of people satisfaction. These measures were selected by taking into account the Mission and Values of the organisation and the approaches deployed.

They include training days, sickness and absentee levels. Targets have been set and trends are available over a five-year period showing the achievement of these targets.

External comparisons are also available for all measures, obtained for local companies in the area. They are readily available from literature sources.

The results show a favourable comparison with the business' own targets and the results have been consistently better than the external comparisons.

- The selected performance measures are appropriate for the organisation.

- The measures have targets, which are met, and link to the Mission and Values.

Criterion 7

The Excellence Model

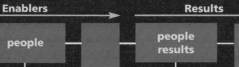

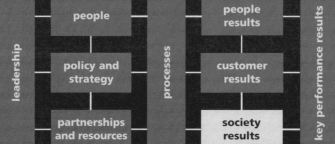

Criterion 8

"The organisation's achievements with respect to society and the local community, based on their opinions and the organisation's measures."

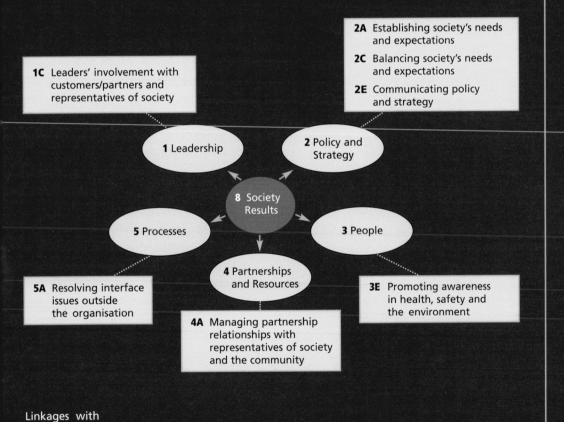

2A Establishing society's needs and expectations

2C Balancing society's needs and expectations

2E Communicating policy and strategy

1C Leaders' involvement with customers/partners and representatives of society

1 Leadership

2 Policy and Strategy

8 Society Results

5 Processes

3 People

4 Partnerships and Resources

5A Resolving interface issues outside the organisation

4A Managing partnership relationships with representatives of society and the community

3E Promoting awareness in health, safety and the environment

Linkages with the enablers

3.8 | Society Results

W hat the organisation is achieving in relation to local, national and international society as appropriate.

Sub-criterion 8A:
Perception measures.

Areas to address may include:

- *Performance as a responsible citizen – disclosures of information relevant to the community, equal opportunities practices, impact on local and national economies, relationships with relevant authorities, ethical behaviour;*

- *Involvement in the communities where it operates – involvement in education and training, support for medical and welfare provision, support for sport and leisure, voluntary work and philanthropy;*

- *Activities to reduce and prevent nuisance and harm from its operations and/or throughout the life cycle of its products – health risks and accidents, noise and odour, hazards (safety), pollution and toxic emission;*

- *Reporting on activities to assist in the preservation and sustainability of resources – choice of transport, ecological impact, reduction and elimination waste and packaging, substitution of raw materials or other inputs, usage of utilities, e.g. gases, water, electricity, new and recycled materials.*

 PRIVATE SECTOR The company supports the local community through the activities of staff. The support given is both financial and practical to those charities and voluntary organisations with which staff are involved. Feedback is sought from these organisations through an annual survey to understand how they perceive the company's contribution to the local community.

Whilst working with community bodies the company also gathers feedback from them to establish its standing. The company has been cited as a "role model" by a number of these organisations regarding its relationship with the community.

Further methods on capturing information on the views of the community include feedback from staff, comments in the press and the responses from organisers of community-based awards.

- Measures of society's perception of the organisation is collected both formally and informally.

- There is a policy to support, and clear evidence of, active involvement with the local community.

- There are some good results with the company cited as a 'role model'.

Criterion 8

The business has received very favourable press commentary on a number of environmental sustainability projects. It applied for, and gained, Charter Mark status in 1995.

At a more local level there has been positive feedback from teachers and voluntary workers for the business' involvement, e.g. a teaching pack to help pupils understand quality concepts. This particular example also gained recognition from the National Quality Organisation.

 The business has a policy to express its care for the community through charitable support, and it supports two local events in the community every year gaining favourable response. In addition, it sponsors a local football team, providing them with kits and helping at fund-raising events.

The organisation has letters of support from the community for providing work experience for pupils from the local disabled college.

The business offers work placement opportunities to school leavers and has set up a partnership with a local college to develop a training programme for a rolling three-year course that will provide work for the college for the following five years.

- Examples presented indicate a favourable perception of the organisation and its activities by society, both locally and nationally.

- There is strong evidence that the company performs as a responsible member of the community and society.

Criterion 8

3.8 | Society Results

What the organisation is achieving in relation to local, national and international society as appropriate.

Sub-criterion 8B:
Performance indicators.

Areas to address may include:

- *Those listed under sub-criterion 8a;*

- *Handling changes in employment levels;*

- *Press coverage;*

- *Dealings with authorities on issues such as – certification, clearances, import/export, planning, product release;*

- *Accolades and awards received.*

PRIVATE SECTOR

One of the organisation's measures of society's satisfaction is that it contributes 1% of its trading results to projects which improve environmental management and care, as a member of a group of companies known as the 1% club. As part of this on-going commitment, five key environmental goals have been set:

- All product areas to have 50% of new projects with an environmental objective

- All product areas to have an environmental plan

- To support water stewardship projects in every country

- To set up a database of volatile organic compounds (VOCs) usage throughout the business

- All sites to have achieved certification to ISO 14001

Originally 33% of sites had ISO 14000 certification, rising to 66% the following year, and 100% by the end of the next year.

- The organisation has set itself a comprehensive, and demanding, set of internal performance measures and targets, by which to judge its society results.

- A stretching target has already been achieved.

Criterion 8

An internal measure of society results is the organisation's proactive approach to downsizing, and positive investment in retraining and redeployment, resulting in almost completely avoiding any compulsory redundancies, despite staff numbers falling by almost 60% in nine years. By providing positive support for the establishment of new community based organisations taking over the organisation's business, it has helped sustain and improve the social infrastructure in these areas.

Several projects have been developed in partnership with other businesses, e.g. to assist unemployed people to find work via apprenticeships and a home to rent on completion of the training, sponsorship of training and the provision of pre-employment training and work experience.

In recent years, the business has won 11 of the 19 regional awards and 26 of the 45 commendations for its projects.

- There are clear measures and results of the positive handling of changes in employment levels.

- There is evidence of a policy to engage in value-adding partnerships with other businesses for the benefit of society.

 The site monitors all key aspects of waste including water, noise, fumes, oil and solvent content. All non-conformances are investigated and reported on. The rate of use of a particular chemical was monitored and the recent conversion to a substitute (in advance of the Montreal Protocol deadline) has resulted in a radical step change and the chemical is now not used at all.

Utility consumption levels are controlled by a computerised 'Building Management System', supported by factory insulation initiatives, plus a computerised preventative maintenance programme, to ensure fuel efficiency is optimised. Checks are made on water consumption to eliminate any underground leaks. Inspections by the Environmental Health Officers confirm on-going compliance. In the last four years the site has been awarded a Royal Society for the Prevention of Accidents (ROSPA) "Gold" Award for Occupational Safety.

- There is evidence of significant step change improvements to minimise the organisation's impact on the local community.

- The site has a recognised record of high and improved safety standards.

Criterion 8

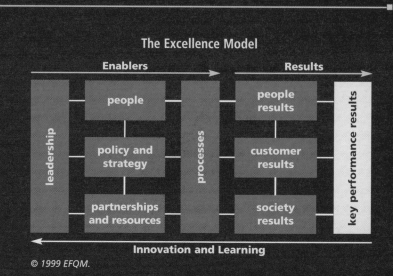

The Excellence Model

Enablers

Results

leadership

people

policy and strategy

partnerships and resources

processes

people results

customer results

society results

key performance results

Innovation and Learning

© 1999 EFQM.

"The organisation's achievements, both financial and non-financial, covering results that are planned and operational measures that are used to monitor and predict."

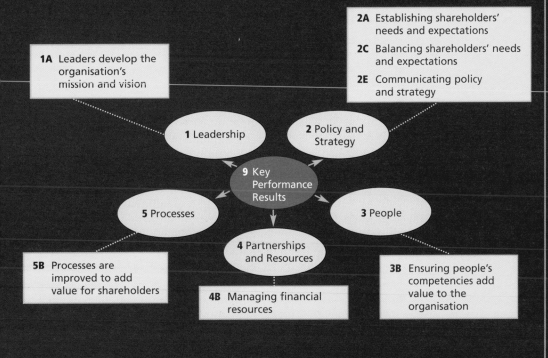

2A Establishing shareholders' needs and expectations

2C Balancing shareholders' needs and expectations

2E Communicating policy and strategy

1A Leaders develop the organisation's mission and vision

1 Leadership

2 Policy and Strategy

9 Key Performance Results

5 Processes

3 People

4 Partnerships and Resources

5B Processes are improved to add value for shareholders

4B Managing financial resources

3B Ensuring people's competencies add value to the organisation

Linkages with the enablers

3.9 | Key Performance Results

What the organisation is achieving in relation to its planned performance.

Sub-criterion 9A:
Key performance outcomes.

Areas to address may include:

- *Financial outcomes including – share price, dividends, gross margins, net profit, sales, meeting of budgets;*

- *Non-financial outcomes including – market share, time to market, volumes, success rates.*

Total business turnover has more than doubled in one year and trading profit has more than trebled in two years. Gross margins, net proceeds on sales, advertising and promotional expense all show significant increases and earnings per share have also shown consistent growth over this period. 85% of the goals from the Plan have been achieved or exceeded.

The business is the market leader in four of its eight product areas, and second in three others. One product was launched in six countries and heralded as a breakthrough innovation, creating a marketing edge over most competitors.

Each product area shows strong growth in both net proceeds on sales and market share, showing that in a relatively static market, growth is being achieved at the expense of competitors.

Benchmark data for key financial indicators show steady and consistent volume growth.

- The business judges its success using a comprehensive and balanced set of financial measures.

- It has demonstrated outstanding performance against its targets and plan.

Criterion 9

A system of unit cost measures is used to continually assess efficiency. Over the last five years, unit cost performance has, each year, exceeded the target set.

Although overall spend on publicity has decreased, the active client base has doubled to 102 over five years. This trend is due to increased marketing, sourcing new customers, identifying new business opportunities and improved performance on tenders.

A key business objective is to ensure that the group breaks even as an overall business. The core business has achieved this throughout the last five years. However, the acquisition of another group during the period resulted in year end losses, because the acquired group brought with it substantial historical losses.

- Positive trends in key performance outcomes over a five-year period are visible and comparisons with targets are favourable.

Sales have grown consistently for 17 years, with exceptional growth in the last year.

Profit has increased by over 250% over a six-year period, whilst the margin has increased from 14% to 21%, net assets have more than doubled, and stock holding has decreased by 17% in the same period.

There is a dramatic achievement in the seasonal profile that the sector and business typically endure – the peak season revenue has tripled in the six-year period, and the low season is now a substantial trading period.

- Results can be linked to planned improvement exercises, and Policy and Strategy decisions.
- Any dips in profits are due to either a planned investment, or to unavoidable external forces affecting the whole sector.
- There is a good balance between investment and profit, plus constant improvement to the business' equipment and premises.

Criterion 9

3.9 | Key Performance Results

What the organisation is achieving in relation to its planned performance.

Sub-criterion 9B:
Key performance indicators.

Areas to address may include:

- *Processes – performance, deployment, assessments, innovations, improvements, cycle times, defect rate, maturity, productivity, time to market;*

- *External resources including partnerships – supplier performance, supplier price, number and value added of partnerships, number and value added of innovative products and services solutions generated by partners, number and value added of joint improvements with partners, recognition of partners' contribution;*

- *Financial – cash flow items, balance sheet items, depreciation, maintenance costs, return on equity, return on net assets, credit ratings;*

- *Buildings, equipment and materials – defect rates, inventory turnover, utility consumption, utilisation;*

- *Technology – innovation rate, value of intellectual property, patents, royalties;*

- *Information and knowledge – accessibility, integrity, relevance, timeliness, sharing and using knowledge, value of intellectual capital.*

 PRIVATE SECTOR The balanced scorecard tracks, as well as financial and stakeholder measures, other key metrics critical to business such as internal measures. Our self-assessment scores against the Model are included in the "Learning and Growth" quadrant. Productivity measures show good performance over the last seven years compared with targets and benchmarks. These measures include:

- Faults repaired per engineer per day

- Faults by objective time and appointment

- Orders completed in six days

- Jobs per engineer per day

- Supplier view of effectiveness of relationship

- Stock turn.

The target of completing 95 % of customer orders within six days has been exceeded for three years and has been better than its benchmark.

- There is a comprehensive set of upstream performance indicators, that are compared with targets and benchmarks.

- Most predictors show good performance compared with targets and benchmarks.

- The approach is enhanced by use of the balanced scorecard tool.

Criterion 9

Performance indicators include those to cover the service provided to customers and suppliers or are measures of efficiency, e.g. paid supplier invoices, processing customer invoices, progress in quality against the indexes of service, product and price, and the number of suppliers producing three or more jobs annually.

The number of supplier invoices paid within the 30 days has risen from 84% to over 98% in a two-year period, due to the work of Quality Action Teams. In the same period, the time taken to process client invoices fell from 11.2 to 10.3 days, and positive trends have been achieved in the quality of service, products and price.

In addition, favourable results have been obtained for some of these measures in a benchmarking exercise with the organisation's group.

- The performance measures include key stakeholders – suppliers and customers.

- There are positive trends in all the predictors measured, and evidence of improvement activities.

 Fixed assets and balance sheet values have increased in two years, by over 400% and 200%, respectively. The business has continued to invest and expand its asset base, including a purpose-built manufacturing facility and equipment, resulting in a doubling of throughput capacities and a reduction in maintenance costs.

Lead-times for key accounts have been reduced by over 70% in a three-year period, and dispatch on time has increased from 40% to over 70%. Defect rates have decreased from 1.1% to 0.6%.

A doubling of capacity, improved quality of product, increase in throughput and a reduction in operating expenses has been achieved after an innovative addition to the manufacturing process as a result of three years of research.

- The business measures performance indicator in several key operational areas.

- There are sustained positive trends in these measures, and evidence of improvements in the areas of process, financial and technology.

Criterion 9

Appendix A1

 ### Private Sector Companies

Agilent Technology (formerly Hewlett Packard):
A division of Hewlett Packard concerned with the design, manufacture and supply of electronic medical equipment.

Barclays Direct Loan Service:
Part of the Barclays Group, employing 644 people and providing phone-a-loan and postal loan service to both Barclays and non-Barclays customers.

BAE SYSTEMS (PROGRAMMES):
Formerly British Aerospace Military Aircraft and Aerostructures, employing over 18,000 people and designing, developing, manufacturing and supporting military aircraft, aircraft structures and associated systems.

BT Payphones:
With a total of 2,038 employees, its business areas are public street payphones, service payphones on privately owned sites and supplying and renting payphones.

DHL International (UK) Limited:
Providing express, door-to-door distribution world-wide, including the overnight delivery of light to medium weight freight and documentation within Europe; employing over 3,500 staff.

NatWest Insurance Services:
A wholly owned subsidiary of National Westminster Bank plc, employing 1,315 staff, and providing general insurance and independent financial advice.

NatWest Mortgage Services:
Provides residential mortgage finance and employs 1,600 staff.

Nortel:
A division of the Canadian company Northern Telecom Limited. Nortel employs 900 people and supplies networked communications solutions to telecommunications service providers.

Post Office Counters:
Employs 12,300 staff. Services include benefit payment, corporate banking, personal banking, savings, insurance, bill payment, bureau de change, mails, telecommunications, lotteries and stationery.

Yellow Pages:
Providing independent advertising, in catalogue and electronic form, for all sectors of business.

Unilever HPC-E:
The European division of Unilever which develops, manufactures and markets products for home and personal care. Brands include Persil, Sure, Lynx, Jif, Organics and Comfort.

 ### Public Sector Organisations

Civil Service College :
As the largest management school in the country, provides training and development to managers and specialists in government.

Central Office of Communication Publications Group:
An executive agency commissioning print and publishing services, and producing a wide range of publications – annual reports, periodicals, White Papers, leaflets, posters and web sites.

Devon Social Services:
Part of Devon County Council with responsibility for the welfare of the people in Devon, and working with other organisations to provide a range of both counselling and practical services to meet individual needs.

DERA:
A part of the Ministry of Defence responsible for technological developments.

DSS IT Services Agency:
Provides information systems and information technology services to support social security provision.

Employment Services South West:
An Agency within the Department for Education and Employment, helping people to find work and employers to fill their vacancies. It is one of nine regions making up the national Employment Service in Britain.

Foxdenton School and Integrated Nursery:
A state primary school for children aged between 2 and 11, catering primarily for those with special educational needs arising from physical or medical difficulties.

HM Customs and Excise, London Central Collection:
Collection of VAT from employers and traders in the London region.

Humberside Police E Division:
Protects, helps and re-assures the people of Humberside. Reduces crime and the fear of crime in partnership with other agencies.

Inland Revenue Accounts Office, Cumbernauld:
Has responsibility for tax collection, banking and accounting of tax and national insurance contributions.

Inland Revenue NICO Insolvency Group:
An executive agency within the DSS with responsibility for national insurance contributions.

Runshaw College:
A tertiary college providing both A levels and vocational course to adults and school leavers, serving over 20,000 students.

Scottish Homes:
A national housing agency enabling the effective provision of good quality housing and to stimulate self-motivated communities.

Appendix A1 (continued)

 ### SMEs and Divisional Units

Aeroquip Aerospace Division:
A business employing around 80 people, responsible for designing, manufacturing and supplying fluid handling products to the UK aerospace original equipment manufacturers.

AP Acrefair:
Air Product's European manufacturing facility employing around 285 people and manufacturing key items of cryogenic plant.

Ducker Engineering:
A small business which manufactures, installs and services equipment for the garment sector of the industrial laundry market, producing on-hanger finishing, sorting, folding and transportation systems for the work wear rental sector.

Lawson Mardon Plastics:
The business employs around 150 people and designs and manufactures injection moulded packaging for the food, beverage, cosmetics and healthcare industries.

Seaview Hotel and Restaurant:
An independent owner-managed, small seaside hotel comprising 16 bedrooms, 2 restaurants and 2 bars, with a workforce of 40, serving both the year-round local and tourist trade.

Springfarm Architectural Mouldings Ltd:
A privately owned company employing 54 people, manufacturing a range of architectural mouldings for the construction and DIY industries, which are sold through builders merchants.

Vista Optics Limited:
A privately owned company with 17 employees, manufacturing medical device polymers for intra-ocular and contact lenses.

Appendix A2

References

Assessing Business Excellence –
L.J. Porter and S.J. Tanner,
Butterworth-Heinemann, 1998.

Award Winning Documents (available from the BQF):

- *BAe, Military Aircraft and Aerostructures*
- *NatWest Insurance Services*
- *Foxdenton School*
- *ICL High Performance Technology*
- *BT Northern Ireland*
- *Mortgage Express*

Quality –
Noriaki Kano et al., Union of Japanese Scientists and Engineers, Tokyo, April 1983.

The Quality 60, A Guide for Service and Manufacturing –
John Bicheno, PICSIE Books, 1998.

Available from the British Quality Foundation:

- *The X-Factor: Winning Performance Through Business Excellence –*
  BQF, 1998.

- *The EFQM Excellence Model –*
  Companies Version,
  ISBN 90-5236-360-9.

- *The EFQM Excellence Model –*
  Public and voluntary sector.
  ISBN 90-5236-369-2

- *The Eight Essentials of Excellence –*
  ISBN 90-5236-077-4.

- *Assessing for Excellence.*
  GSA 9A

Appendix A3

Glossary of Terms to Help with Use and Understanding of the EFQM Excellence Model

Creativity
The generation of ideas for new or improved working practices and/or products and services.

Culture
The total range of behaviours, ethics and values that are transmitted, practised and reinforced by members of the organisation.

Enablers
Enabler criteria are concerned with how the organisation approaches each of the activities suggested by the criterion parts.

Ethics
The universal morals that the organisation adopts and abides by.

Excellence
Outstanding practice in managing the organisation and achieving results based on fundamental concepts.

External Customers
The end customers of the organisation. These may also include other customers in the distribution chain (see also internal customers).

Finances
The short-term funds required for the day-to-day operation, and the capital funding required for the longer term financing, of the organisation.

Innovation
The practical translation of ideas into new products, services, processes, systems and social interactions.

Internal Customers
The recipients of the outputs of processes within an organisation.

Knowledge
Part of the hierarchy of data, information and knowledge. Data is raw facts; information is data with context and perspective; knowledge is information with guidance for action.

Leaders
The people who co-ordinate and balance the interests of all who have a stake in the organisation, including the executive team, all other managers and those in team leadership positions or with a subject leadership role.

Learning
The acquiring and understanding of information which may lead to improvement or change. Organisational learning activities include benchmarking, assessments, audits and best practice studies. Individual learning activities include training and professional qualifications.

Management System
The framework of processes and procedures used to ensure that the organisation can fulfil all tasks required to achieve its objectives.

Mission
A statement that describes the purpose of an organisation – why it exists.

Partnerships
A working relationship between two or more parties creating added value for the customer. Partners can include suppliers, distributors, joint ventures and alliances.

People
All of the individuals employed by the organisation, including full-time, part-time, contract and temporary employees.

Perception
The opinion of an individual or group of people.

Performance
A measure of attainment achieved by an individual, team, organisation or process.

Process
A sequence of activities that adds value by producing required outputs from a variety of inputs.

RADAR®
Results, Approach, Deployment, Assessment and Review.

Results
Result criteria are concerned with what the organisation has achieved or is achieving.

Stakeholders
All those who have an interest in an organisation, its activities and achievements. These may include customers, partners, employees, shareholders, owners, government and regulators.

Society
All those who are, or believe they are, affected by an organisation, other than its people, customers and partners.

Values
The understandings and expectations that describe how the organisation's people behave and upon which all business relationships are based, e.g. trust, support and truth.

Vision
A statement that describes how the organisation wishes to be in the future.